the VAN DIEMEN
ANTHOLOGY 2023

THE VAN DIEMEN HISTORY PRIZE

Writing and history have long been lovers, both needing and complementing each other. Non-fiction can make for compelling reading, no matter what the subject, and this is arguably truest when the subject is history. One has only to look at the books—and the sales figures—of Dava Sobel about longitude and Simon Singh about mathematics to see that the work of historians and the art of good writing are natural partners.

It is that collaboration, that love affair, that The Van Diemen History Prize celebrates.

—Chris Champion,
Editor, *Forty South Tasmania* magazine

the VAN DIEMEN ANTHOLOGY 2023

the best of
the VAN DIEMEN
HISTORY PRIZE 2022–2023

selected by
Tony Fenton, Dr Kristyn Harman,
Kirstie Ross and Chris Champion

© 2023
Copyright remains with the individual authors

ISBN 978-0-6457367-8-6

All rights reserved.

Without limiting the rights under copyright above, no part of this publication may be reproduced, stored in or introduced into a retrieval system, or transmitted in any form or by any means (electronic, mechanical, photocopying, recording or otherwise), without the prior written permission of the relevant author.

Anatomy of a Scandal: An earlier version of this article first appeared in Issue 14 of *Traces*, March 2021. It has been expanded upon with the editor's knowledge and permission.

Published by Forty South Publishing Pty Ltd, Hobart, Tasmania
www.fortysouth.com.au

Printed by IngramSpark

Cover image: Carnarvon Town Hall or Convict Asylum Clock Tower (detail)
Sarah White

Title page image: London Docks by Henry Moses, 1824 (detail).
Part two of Moses' 'Sketches of Shipping'. Reproduced with permission, Green Blackwall collection, Royal Museums Greenwich, PAD7901

CONTENTS

    Competition judges   vi
    Anthology contributors   viii

Philippa Moore   1
    Anatomy of a scandal
    A love triangle in 1820s Hobart Town

Terry Mulhern   10
    A difficult birth
    The Van Diemen's Land Company, 1824–25

Melanie Roylance   20
    Frank Pogson Bethune
    Tasmania's warrior priest

Ray Bassett   32
    Gold amongst the tin

Carla Baker   40
    Mysterious broken binding proves a silver lining

Anne Lee-Archer   47
    Theatre Royal Hobart
    The architectural influence of William Gore Elliston,
    John Lee Archer and Samuel Beazley
    and their passion for the Arts

Guy Salvidge   61
    "Pardoned to serve His Majesty by sea"
    The life of George Briggs

Sarah White   72
    Port Arthur or Carnarvon
    The changing landscape of a former penal settlement

COMPETITION JUDGES

TONY FENTON majored in Physics and Computer Science at the University of Tasmania and completed a Graduate Diploma in Information Management. Following a period of work for the State Library of Tasmania, he has devoted most of his time to historical research and writing. His long-standing interest in South West Tasmania—brought about by his grandfather, the legendary tin-miner and naturalist Deny King—led to an exhaustive study of the history of Port Davey. Tony's first book, *A History of Port Davey, Southwest Tasmania, Volume 1: Fleeting Hopes* (Forty South Publishing, 2017) was shortlisted in the inaugural Dick and Joan Green Family Award for Tasmanian History in 2018 and longlisted in the 2017 Tasmanian Literary Prizes, Margaret Scott Prize. As a finalist in the inaugural Van Diemen History Prize, his essay "Eclipse" was highly commended. In the 2020–2021 Van Diemen History Prize he was joint winner (alongside Terry Mulhern) with his essay "Unsafe Harbour".

DR KRISTYN HARMAN is an Associate Professor in History and the Deputy Chair of Academic Senate at the University of Tasmania. Her research interests cohere around socio-cultural frontiers including transportation to, and within, British colonies; frontier warfare; Indigenous incarceration; and the Australian and New Zealand home fronts during World War Two. She is the author of *Cleansing the Colony: Transporting Convicts from New Zealand to Van Diemen's Land* (2017), longlisted for the Royal Society Te Aparangi Award in the Ockham New Zealand Book Awards, 2018. In 2014, Kristyn won the Australian Historical Association Kay Daniels award for her first book, *Aboriginal Convicts: Australian, Khoisan, and Māori Exiles* (2012). Kristyn's work is represented in top tier journals including the *Journal of Colonialism and Colonial History*, and the *Journal of Imperial and Commonwealth History*.

KIRSTIE ROSS is a curator and historian with over 20 years' experience, working in the heritage sector on both sides of the Tasman. At the time of judging the prize she was Senior Curator of Cultural Heritage at the Tasmanian Museum and Art Gallery in Hobart, a Director on the West Coast Heritage Centre's Board and a member of the Australian Dictionary of Biography Tasmanian Working Group. Since June 2023, Kirstie has been Head Curator, Published and Special Collections at the University of Otago's Hocken Collection in Dunedin, New Zealand. Kirstie's research and writing concentrates on 20th century social history topics, which she enjoys sharing in diverse ways, including Instagram, blogs, exhibitions, radio interviews, as well as academic publications. In 2004 she co-authored the illustrated book *Holding on to Home: New Zealand Stories and Objects of the Great War*. A highlight of her career was leading the team that curated the award-winning exhibition *Gallipoli: The Scale of Our War,* at the Museum of New Zealand, which was a collaboration with Academy Award winner, Sir Richard Taylor.

CHRIS CHAMPION is editor of *Forty South Tasmania* magazine and a director of Forty South Publishing with responsibility for all editorial functions. He has worked as an editor in Australia and Asia for more than 40 years. The historians on the judging panel assessed all entries and created a short list based on the merit of their historical investigation and writing quality. Chris then chose the winners based on writing quality.

ANTHOLOGY CONTRIBUTORS

PHILIPPA MOORE is a PhD candidate in creative writing and history at the University of Tasmania. She is fascinated by the hidden stories of women, particularly from the nineteenth and twentieth centuries. Philippa has worked in Melbourne, London and now Hobart as a journalist, editor and copywriter, with her work appearing in *Womankind*, *The Guardian*, *Elle*, *Cosmopolitan* and others. Her first book, *The Latte Years* (Black Inc, 2016), reflects on her time as a popular and award-winning blogger in the medium's formative years, pre-social media—it started life as a novel but was eventually published as a memoir. Philippa's PhD project, a novel inspired by the life of convict entrepreneur Maria Lord, has received a 2023 KSP Residential Fellowship. In her writing, and especially in her current research at UTAS, Philippa very much enjoys traversing the blurry borders between fiction and facts.

TERRY MULHERN is a writer and academic who splits his time between Somerset in northwest Tasmania and Melbourne. Terry's writing spans themes of Tasmanian history, ecology, and culture.

Terry was joint winner (with Tony Fenton) of 2020/21 Van Diemen History Prize with his essay "Insubordination and Improper Intimacy". His 2018/19 entry, "St Valentine's Tears" was highly commended. He has also published in *Forty South Tasmania*, *Science Write Now*, *Pursuit* and the *Papers and Proceedings of the Royal Society of Tasmania*. His short stories "The Flying Fish" and "The Satchel" were finalists in the 2022 and 2021 Tasmanian Writer's Prizes. For more of Terry's writing see www.terrymulhern.com.

Born in north Queensland, Terry has worked at universities in the UK and around Australia, but he only feels truly at home in the northwest.

RAY BASSETT has no writing accolades to vaunt, bar a published poem three decades ago and several years as a "rock journalist" for a '90s street magazine. His principal occupation is musician masquerading as a forklift driver, which has been a lot since the virus. He shares a house with his guitars and books in the northwest of Melbourne. An expat Tasmanian, Ray's artistic endeavours have often drawn on his affection for the West Coast of Tasmania. In the last decade that affection has become something of an amateur research project. When not otherwise engaged, Ray is a frequent traveller around Victoria taking sound samples and photographs.

CARLA BAKER is passionate about Tasmania, her family and cultural history. Her Honours thesis, completed at the University of Tasmania in 2021, focused on Mrs W Fletcher's folios. She was the recipient of a UTAS Humanities in Place Industry Engagement Scholarship to undertake this project, which was awarded First Class Honours. Carla is currently a first year History PhD candidate at UTAS with her research investigating the notions of the centre and periphery, and race and purity, using Northern Tasmanian apples as an exemplar. Carla also works in the family-owned mower and chainsaw shop and is mum to two beautiful girls.

ANNE LEE-ARCHER runs her own marketing consulting business in real life, but she would ideally love to give up her day job and research and write history. She has a particular interest in architectural and engineering history, but she also enjoys delving into the connections between people to glean greater insight into a particular time. Her interest in theatre and the arts started with learning music at the age of five. She later attained her A.Mus.A and Associate in Music with the Yamaha Foundation. She has worked for national arts organisations and consults now to arts clients, Her great-great-grandfather was John Lee Archer, Civil Engineer, who laid the foundation stone of the Theatre Royal, Hobart.

MELANIE ROYLANCE is a Brisbane-based writer and recent graduate of the University of Tasmania. After retiring from the corporate rat-race seven years ago, Melanie fulfilled her long-held promise to herself to go back to university to study Australian History. With a life-long interest in genealogy, she is interested in the effect of key historical events on individuals, families, and communities. Melanie's recent Honours thesis investigated the impact of World War I on the people living in the Tasmanian Central Highlands municipality of Hamilton. Currently, she is researching the lives of Australian war widows in the inter-war years for her PhD at the University of Queensland.

GUY SALVIDGE's intermittently award-winning fiction has appeared in *Westerly, Award Winning Australian Writing* and *Stories of Perth*. His most recent published novel is *Complicity City*. Guy is currently undertaking a PhD in

Creative Writing at Curtin University, for which he is writing a novel, *Diemens*, set in early colonial Tasmania. Non-fiction pieces related to his research have appeared in *Backstory*, *Traces* and *Saltbush Review*. When he's not writing, Guy moonlights as an English teacher in rural Western Australia.

SARAH WHITE graduated from Deakin University with a Bachelor of Arts, majoring in Journalism and Literary Studies, and from the University of New England with a Master of History degree. Her work has previously been published in both a local anthology and a national academic journal. Sarah enjoys exploring history through the eyes of those who lived in the past. While she's a fan of empirical, data driven evidence, her favourite thing is to become absorbed in the words of first-hand accounts. She'll often be found lost in the archives.

JOINT WINNER, THE VAN DIEMEN HISTORY PRIZE 2022–2023

Anatomy of a scandal

A love triangle in 1820s Hobart Town

PHILIPPA MOORE

This essay is dedicated, in loving memory, to Valerie Browne Lester (1939–2019)

In December 1824, the newly-formed Supreme Court of Van Diemen's Land was occupied with a case so engrossing and the evidence for which was so "filthy and disgusting"[1] that it took 14 days—some where the court sat for up to 17 hours at a time—for a verdict to be reached.

The case was *Lord v Rowcroft*, a trial of criminal conversation, which is a civil tort that could be invoked by a husband against any man who had sexual intercourse with his wife. A charge could be brought regardless of whether the encounter (or indeed encounters) was consensual, for there was not much difference where the law was concerned. Women were considered the property of their husbands and any interference with that property could be perceived to result in a loss "excessive to the husband".[2] Criminal conversation was formally abolished from the British legal system in 1857 with the introduction of the *Divorce Act* and is largely extinct in modern legal systems, but "crim.con" cases were common in late 18th and early 19th century England, with injured husbands seeking settlements of thousands of pounds "for the loss of male honour incurred through the seduction of a wife".[3]

Lord v Rowcroft is also illustrative of a curious turning point for the colony of Van Diemen's Land, where several decades of corruption and permissive behaviour—such as openly cavorting with other people's spouses, something many of the Governors had done—were coming to an end. A sexual scandal such as this had the potential to be a propagandist tool to discredit the reputation of the colony itself and Hobart Town's citizens, whether well-established or newly arrived, were finding that respectability was a "weapon to be wielded in the small politics of everyday life".[4]

The woman at the centre of the scandal, Maria Lord, was a silent figure in the courtroom, unsurprisingly. At the time of the trial, she had been living in Hobart Town for nearly 20 years. Her move to Van Diemen's Land had been under interesting circumstances: Maria Riseley, as she was known then, originally came to Sydney on the ship The Experiment in 1804 after being sentenced to seven years' transportation for stealing almost a year's salary's worth of goods from her employer. After working briefly as an assigned domestic servant, Maria ended up pregnant and back in the Parramatta Gaol, destined to lose her baby to the orphanage and resign herself to a life of hard labour and limited, if any, freedom. However, her fortunes changed rapidly, and unexpectedly.

Shortly after Maria gave birth to her daughter Caroline, Edward Lord, an officer in the marines and rising star in the government of Van Diemen's Land, turned up at the gaol in search of a "companion". He selected Maria, who immediately agreed to set sail with him, and Caroline, to Hobart Town, where a very different life awaited.

Maria and Edward lived together openly for a few years, welcoming two more children (one of which sadly died in infancy) before she received a pardon from Joseph Foveaux, the Lieutenant-Governor of Norfolk Island (likely as a favour to Edward)[5] and they were married in 1808. Over the next 14 years, another four children were born and Edward and Maria established themselves as land, ship and business owners.

Edward was an ambitious man who craved wealth, but while he worked for the government he was not permitted to trade so it was Maria who took the reins. She set up and ran three general stores in Hobart Town and proved herself to be a skilled and capable businesswoman, eventually managing all her husband's business concerns and effectively controlling the meat, wheat and rum trades in Van Diemen's Land. She handled day-to-day transactions and he was the negotiator, either buttering up the right people in power or away in England, returning with their ships filled with desirable wares to sell in their stores. They owned expansive properties, cargo ships and whaling brigs, and all their children were sent to England to be educated as soon as they were old enough.

But Edward's long absences—often for years at a time—clearly took a toll on their marriage. And despite transcending her lowly beginnings to become one of the colony's wealthiest and most successful women, Maria was never allowed to forget her convict past. "The society here is abominable," wrote Janet Ranken to her sister in England shortly after arriving in Hobart Town in 1821. "Mr Lord a man worth half a million money is married to a convict woman."[6] William Bligh too referred to Maria as "a Convict Woman of infamous character".[7]

Despite her incredible success, or perhaps because of it, it seemed people were just waiting for Maria to fall from grace.

In 1821, 23-year-old Charles Rowcroft arrived in Hobart Town to take up a land grant with his brother. Articulate and Eton-educated, Charles was quickly accepted as a gentleman of the colony and caught the attention of Edward Lord, who enjoyed taking promising new arrivals under his wing. Charles became a regular fixture in their circle, which included Reverend Robert Knopwood, a well-known figure in early Van Diemen's Land and prolific diarist. His diaries note that he dined with Maria regularly while Edward was away on his lengthy business trips, and in 1822, Charles Rowcroft begins to appear in Knopwood's diary as a frequent guest at Maria's table, especially once Edward departed for another long spell abroad.[8] Maria, at age 43, clearly still retained the spirit and beauty which had enticed her husband to select her from a line-up of women in Parramatta some 17 years earlier.

In July 1822, a few months after Edward had sailed for England, Maria put her youngest child, a two-year-old daughter, into a boarding school and took off to Port Dalrymple for a few weeks with Charles.[9] Whatever was going on between them, they weren't hiding it. Perhaps Maria, having long endured prejudice and slights, was beyond caring what anyone thought of her. With Edward gone for years at a time, she may have suspected that he too was enjoying someone else's company. What was good for the goose was good for the gander, surely?

A CULTURAL AND MORAL TURNING POINT

Unfortunately for Maria and Charles, as their affair deepened, things were changing in Van Diemen's Land. The onset of free emigration to the colonies in the 1820s had a significant influence on "improving the morals of the residents"[10] as well as those in power, leading to increased moral surveillance, more consciousness of class, and more social control and exclusion. There was also enhanced government regulation, providing a stark contrast to the early days of Hobart Town, where corruption and dishonesty were rampant and "men soon realised whatever they did, no one was going to stop them, at least in the short term."[11] In 1822, William Sorell had been Lieutenant-Governor for five years and while he had done his best to clean up the mess he had inherited from Thomas Davey, the moral example he set with his private life most likely lessened his influence and achievements. It was common knowledge that Sorell was living openly with a woman he wasn't married to, having left his lawful wife and children behind in Britain to take this prestigious post. With such a man in charge, it is little wonder that Maria and Charles did not take care to conceal their affair.

Sorell was recalled from his position as Lieutenant-Governor in August 1823 and his replacement, George Arthur, "a man of inflexible determination, unceasing energy, and great powers of administration",[12] arrived in Hobart Town in May 1824, signalling a new era in which opportunities for corruption and moral deviance would be drastically reduced if not obliterated. William Parramore, a young clerk in the office of the attorney-general, observed in a letter home that George Arthur had "arrived in the nick of time" and "it is therefore now the interest of all who would stand well with the Gov. to <u>seem</u> moral."[13] Churches were suddenly full every Sunday, so full that new pews had to be built, and any convict living in adultery was now sent back to the penitentiary, a policy that had been difficult to enforce under Sorell.[14] The boundaries of acceptable conduct were shifting. It was not a good time to be in a public love triangle.

Perhaps Maria sensed this. In September 1823, just after Sorell had been recalled and with the storm clouds of her own scandal gathering, she publicly announced in the *Hobart Town Gazette* that she was planning to sail to England.[15] She had many motivations for doing so. She might have wanted to reconcile with Edward and escape the gossip; perhaps she was panicking about the enormous financial losses they were facing with the failure of several shipping expeditions; or maybe she simply wanted to see her children for the first time in years. But whatever her motivations, she didn't end up going. Meanwhile, someone had sent word to Edward of his wife's affair. It is unclear who, but there are many contenders—by now the colony's gentlemen, in light of the town's renewed moral vigour, had turned against Charles and believed Maria should be disgraced and shunned.

On hearing the news, Edward acted quickly. He appointed Dr Samuel Hood as his power of attorney and manager of his concerns, taking those powers off Maria.[16] Edward returned to Hobart Town in late October 1824 and on December 6, in the newly established Supreme Court, he charged Charles Rowcroft with criminal conversation.[17]

THE TRIAL

While there are records of several cases tried in the Court's first year of operation, official records of *Lord v Rowcroft* have not survived. Therefore, only a partial picture of what transpired when the scandal entered the courtroom can be established. The *Hobart Town Gazette* gave updates each week:

> The attenuated trial of Charles Rowcroft, Esq. for crim.con. is still pending in the Supreme Court—the general arrangements of which are consequently interfered with, to the serious inconvenience of His Honor the CHIEF JUSTICE, the Assessors, and the Bar, who have repeatedly since the commencement of this cause sat 8, 10, and even 14 hours, without adjourning for the purposes of refreshment.[18]

The letters of William Parramore also provide an interesting perspective. Unsurprisingly, the way he writes about Maria is laced with prejudice:

> I believe I got my cold in the courthouse where the last fortnight has been acted again the trial of the queen. Edwd Lord Esq JP brought an action against Charles Rowcroft "Esq. JP" for crim. con with his wife. The trial lasted 11 days and there was as much nauseous detail as in the other notorious trial. The same object as was attributed to the king, was said to be the aim of Lord—a divorce from a wife whom he is now ashamed of, because she can't read, and <u>can</u> put herself into most <u>original</u> passions and curse and swear. You must know Lord is a man possessed of the most "property" in the island—but there is a very palpable distinction between "property" and money.[19]

The "other notorious trial" was King George IV attempting to divorce Queen Caroline by introducing the Pains and Penalties Bill of 1820. Because divorce could only be granted by proving adultery—something neither party would admit to—George introduced a bill that would effectively put his wife on trial for adultery and if passed, would declare her guilty and he could obtain the divorce.

Parramore's letter is the only remaining primary source that even hints at what was actually said in the courtroom. Knopwood's commentary on the trial (he was a sitting magistrate) only extends to its extraordinary length and the long days involved; he was appalled that the court sat from 9.30 in the morning until 2.30 the following morning, and only one hour's break was allowed for refreshment.[20] Knopwood was also called as a witness in the trial's final days and, interestingly, he notes he called on Edward Lord the evening before his first day in the witness box.[21]

Why the trial was so lengthy when the verdict was almost a given is a mystery. Similarly mysteriously, publication of a manuscript with all the salacious details of the trial was advertised but never eventuated.[22] The verdict was eventually given on December 18, 1824, in favour of Edward, with £100 damages awarded.[23] This was not much money for a case like this at the time—in 1817, William Sorell had paid £3,000 damages in his own case of criminal conversation—but getting money out of Charles Rowcroft, who was not the man of substance he had led people to believe, was perhaps not the point. Maria had effectively been found guilty of adultery so no longer had any control over or official claim on any assets. Edward had secured control of everything and could return to England and his new partner, with whom he had already had a child, and rest easy, knowing that none of his wealth was "going to find its way into the pockets of a penniless adventurer".[24]

THE AFTERMATH

Divorces were public and expensive so, given Maria and Edward couldn't afford it in any sense of the word, they remained legally married but never lived together again. Maria spent the rest of her life in Tasmania, and Edward settled back in England with his new partner, with whom he had another five children. Several of Maria and Edward's children returned to Hobart in early adulthood, but the majority of them she never saw again. One can only imagine what they were told.

While Maria no longer had the business empire she had enjoyed prior to her affair, when both her husband and her lover left Australia permanently after the trial, she continued to live and work in Hobart Town with her head held high. In fact, she appears to have been on the receiving end of kindness, support and even some sympathy and understanding, as her notice in the *Hobart Town Gazette* not even a year later suggests:[25]

> MRS. MARIA LORD, in returning Thanks for the very kind and liberal Support which she has received in her Endeavours to obtain a future Support for herself and her Children, begs leave to acquaint her Friends and the Public, that she has opened her Stores at the corner of Elizabeth and Liverpool-streets; where she has for SALE, on Commission, British and Foreign Goods of all Descriptions.—For the convenience of Agricultural Settlers, a Butcher's Shop is established on the Premises, to receive Meat in Payment for Goods; Money also, if preferred, will be given for Meat, at all Times, on the the most liberal Conditions.
> MRS. MARIA LORD will continue to receive Goods for Sale on Commission; and she trusts that the Experience of the whole Colony, of her Integrity and Assiduity in Business for the last Sixteen Years, will be sufficient Guarantee for her future Exertions.

However, society did not restore Maria's respectability the way it did for some of her contemporaries, such as fellow entrepreneur and convict Mary Reibey. If things had been different, perhaps it would be Maria's face on the $20 note today. Instead, no confirmed likeness of her remains in existence. Despite her many achievements and quite public life, the scandal and ensuing trial returned her to a lowlier status and resulted in her being condemned to historical obscurity, as so many convict women were.

As for Charles Rowcroft, a fresh start was sorely needed. He couldn't pay the damages of £100 so his property was transferred to Edward. After hearing of the death of his father, who was the British Ambassador to Peru, Charles left Van Diemen's Land for good in 1825. On his ship was Janett Curling, a widow with five children, whom Charles married when the vessel docked at Rio de Janeiro. Charles and his new family returned to England and in 1843, his first novel *Tales of the Colonies, or, the Adventures of an Emigrant, Edited by a late Colonial Magistrate*, was published. It was the first novel to depict emigration to Australia. Charles died mysteriously at sea in 1856. Maria outlived him, by only three years. Doubtless the lovers never reunited, but perhaps there was a letter (or two) that somehow found its way across continents. They had, after all, sacrificed everything to be together, once.

Maria ran several businesses—a smaller general store, a boarding house and a butcher's shop—in Hobart Town after the scandal and then she retired to Bothwell, not far from where Charles had previously owned land at Norwood on the Clyde River. Perhaps she had a fondness for the area, and those carefree days with her young lover had been some of the happiest of her life. I like to think of her, taking tea on the terrace of the grand house where she lived for her final years, looking into the distance, remembering him and smiling.

■ ■ ■

NOTES

1. James Thomson to George Arthur, December 16, 1824. Colonial Secretary's Office General Correspondence (CSO1), CSO01/1/91/2098, Tasmanian Archives and Heritage Office, Hobart.
2. *Hart v Bowman*. 1828. NSWSupC 104.
3. Lawrence Stone, *Road to Divorce: England 1530–1987* (Oxford, 1990: online edn, Oxford Academic, October 3, 2011), 296.
4. Kirsten McKenzie. "Discourses of Scandal: Bourgeois Respectability and the End of Slavery and Transportation at the Cape and New South Wales, 1830–1850", *Journal of Colonialism and Colonial History* 4, no. 3 (2003) doi:10.1353/cch.2004.0011, accessed July 1, 2022.
5. William Bligh to Lord Castlereagh, June 10, 1809, in *Historical records of Australia. Series I, Governors' despatches to and from England*. Volume 7, 1809–13. (Sydney: Library Committee of the Commonwealth Parliament, 1914–1925), 128–29.
6. Janet Ranken to Margaret Hutchinson, December 1821, in Patricia Clarke and Dale Spender (eds), *Lifelines: Australian women's letters and diaries, 1788–1840* (Sydney: Allen & Unwin, 1992), 152.
7. Bligh to Castlereagh, June 10, 1809, 129.
8. Robert Knopwood, *The diary of the Reverend Robert Knopwood, 1803–1838: first Chaplain of Van Diemen's Land*, ed. Mary Nicholls (Hobart: Tasmanian Historical Research Association, 1977), 357–58, 361–62.
9. Knopwood, *Diary*, 367.
10. *The Cyclopedia of Tasmania (Illustrated): an historical and commercial review, descriptive and biographical, facts, figures, and illustrations; an epitome of progress, business men and commercial interests* (Ballarat: Maitland and Krone, 1900), 178; https://stors.tas.gov.au/25841, accessed February 8, 2021.

11. Alison Alexander, *Corruption and Skullduggery: Edward Lord, Maria Riseley and Hobart's tempestuous beginnings* (Hobart: Pillinger Press, 2015), 150.
12. *The Cyclopedia of Tasmania*, 46.
13. William Parramore to Thirza Cropper, October 7, 1824, in DC Shelton (Ed), *The Parramore Letters: Written from Van Diemen's Land, 1823–1825* (Privately published, Epping, NSW, 1993), 53.
14. Parramore to Cropper, October 7, 1824, 53–54.
15. *Hobart Town Gazette and Van Diemen's Land Advertiser*, September 6, 1823, 1; https://trove.nla.gov.au/newspaper/article/1089962, accessed September 7, 2022.
16. *Hobart Town Gazette and Van Diemen's Land Advertiser*, August 9, 1823, 2; https://trove.nla.gov.au/newspaper/article/1089943, and August 6, 1824, 1; https://trove.nla.gov.au/newspaper/article/1090287, accessed September 7, 2022
17. Knopwood, *Diary*, 436.
18. *Hobart Town Gazette and Van Diemen's Land Advertiser*, December 17, 1824, 2; https://trove.nla.gov.au/newspaper/article/1090433, accessed 7 September 2022.
19. William Parramore to Thirza Cropper, December 20, 1824, in Shelton, 61.
20. Knopwood, *Diary*, 436.
21. Knopwood, *Diary*, 437.
22. *Hobart Town Gazette and Van Diemen's Land Advertiser*, December 10, 1824, 1; https://trove.nla.gov.au/newspaper/page/123471, accessed September 7, 2022.
23. Knopwood, *Diary*, 437.
24. Kay Daniels, *Convict Women* (Sydney: Allen & Unwin, 1998), 22.
25. *Hobart Town Gazette and Van Diemen's Land Advertiser*, August 12, 1825, 1; https://trove.nla.gov.au/newspaper/page/123916, accessed September 7, 2022.

JOINT WINNER, THE VAN DIEMEN HISTORY PRIZE 2022–2023

A difficult birth

The Van Diemen's Land Company, 1824–25

TERRY MULHERN

In the spring of 1825, the City of London was infected with a tropical fever. Securities in Latin American silver and gold mines boomed and share prices soared. Speculation was rife and wild money-making schemes were hatched, such as "... sending Scotch milkmaids to milk the wild cattle of Buenos Ayres".[1] British investors were giddy with their exotic South American "investments". But sharks were circling. Many of these ventures were little more than Ponzi schemes that created the illusion of high returns with little risk, while most of the money was siphoned off. When the bubble burst, London's investors were fleeced.

Around the same time, two Australian joint stock companies were founded, for the purpose of fleecing something else—sheep. The textile mills of northern England were hungry for wool. Their traditional Spanish and Portuguese suppliers were still recovering after the annihilation of their mighty flocks during the Peninsular War a decade earlier. So, Britain's mill owners shifted their eyes outward to the colonies.

In New South Wales, John MacArthur had the foresight to cash in on this opportunity. He first imported merinos from Britain in 1804, but the real boom came later, when the plains of the Central Tablelands were found in 1813 by surveyor George Evans. To fill these "empty" pastures, MacArthur and others imported German fine-woolled merinos. By the start of the 1820s, the economy of New South Wales was well and truly riding on the sheep's back.

During the boom of 1824, MacArthur realised a long-held dream to create a chartered joint stock company so he could dominate Australian wool production. In Britain, a parliamentary Bill and Royal Charter were required to establish a joint stock company and for it to be incorporated. This allowed its shares to be traded and gave it legal status as an entity, protecting the directors from personal legal liability should the company fail. With the gold stamp of an Act of Parliament granting his Australian Agricultural Company 1,000,000 acres, MacArthur easily attracted subscribers in bubble-frenzied London and established £1,000,000 capital to fund his venture.

Chartered joint stock companies have a long history in European colonialism. The most famous example is the Honourable East India Company, which received its charter from Queen Elizabeth I in 1600. Over the next 250 years the East India Company, under its various guises, grew into an empire itself, with its own flag, territories and army. No doubt, this model, which reached its prime in the early 19th century, appealed to MacArthur's Machiavellian inclinations and desire to establish an Australian aristocracy based on trade and wealth.

But MacArthur had competition. On Wednesday, May 12, 1824, 11 gentlemen, including three sitting British MPs, met in London to discuss "proposals for establishing a Company in Van Diemen's Land & for obtaining a Grant of Land there".[2] At this meeting, they consulted John Ingle, "a Gentleman of great experience" who had resided in Van Diemen's Land.

Ingle had accompanied Lieutenant-Governor David Collins on his failed attempt to establish a colony at Port Phillip in 1803. After Collins relocated to the Derwent in 1804, Ingle resigned his administrative post and set himself up as a merchant. He travelled back and forth to England, bringing valuable cargoes he sold in Hobart for a pretty profit. In 1818, Ingle departed Hobart for the last time. Unlike his assigned convicts, Ingle's 14 years in Van Diemen's Land had made him very rich.

At Ingle's meeting with the gentlemen of the VDL Co, he expressed himself " … most decidedly in favour of an establishment for the purpose of cultivating a District of land there". On this basis, and later with the support of the recently returned Lieutenant-Governor of Van Diemen's Land, Colonel William Sorell, the 11 gentlemen pushed ahead with their plan.

Just over a year later, on June 10, 1825, The Van Diemen's Land Company Court of Directors assembled at their offices in Old Broad Street in the City of London to celebrate the passing of the parliamentary bill approving their Royal Charter. But the mood was sombre. In March, share prices had plummeted and there had been a run on bank deposits. Six London banks, and 60 in the

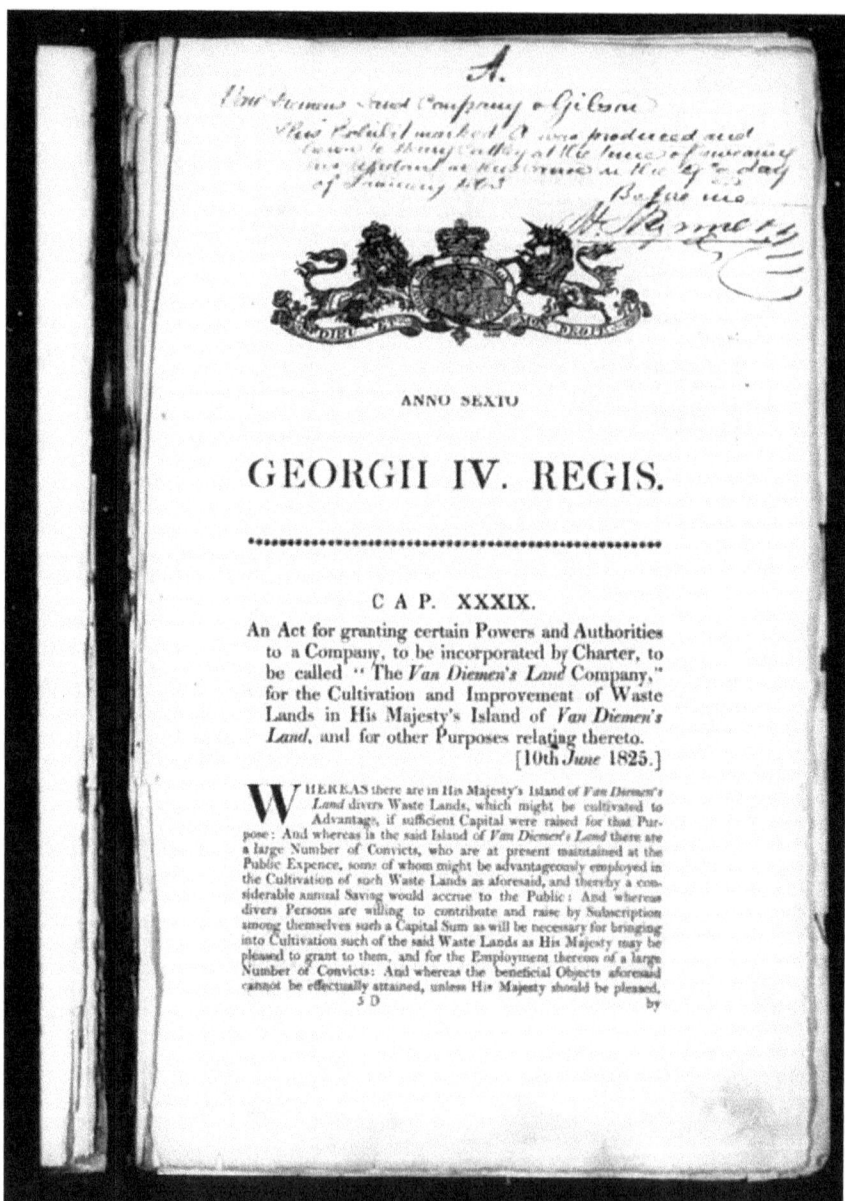

Van Diemen's Land Company Act 1825.

Records of the Van Diemen's Land Company. Reproduced with permission, National Library of Australia, Series M358-M363

Old Broad Street in the City of London.

From *London and its environs in the nineteenth century: illustrated by a series of views from original drawings* by Thomas H Shepherd. Published: London, Jones & Co., 1829. Reproduced with permission. Digitised by The University of California for hathitrust.org.

counties, failed, including the VDL Company's bank, Pole, Thorton, Free, Down & Scott. Luckily, however, this occurred before the Company collected subscriptions from its shareholders and little damage was done to their finances. The directors transferred their banking to the Bank of England, which was still afloat, if only just.

The fledgling Company had survived the panic of 1825, the first stock market crash not caused by war or natural disaster.

In its aftermath, the mood in England swung against "the moral debasement, which exists in all money speculations".[3] When a bill to establish another joint stock company came before the House of Lords, The Lord High Chancellor, Lord Eldon, railed against the speculative nature of these companies, which he described as "evil", as well as the unjust power they wielded in the market. He said, "The result would be a monopoly which would be destructive to all competition!"[4]

When the VDL Co was first mooted during the heady times of 1824, its plans were much grander than what eventually passed parliament. The Colonial Secretary, Lord Bathurst, and his under-secretary, Sir Robert

Wilmot-Horton, were wary of creating a monster. Firstly, the Company's request for 500,000 acres was slashed in half. Even so, in Van Diemen's Land, Andrew Bent, editor of the *Colonial Times* and burr under the saddle of the establishment, raged against the Company's 250,000 acres as "An immense Grant of Land, wholly disproportioned to the geographical dimensions of this Island", fearing the Company would "ruin all private competitions", as no individual landholder "could stand against the prodigious power" of such an entity.[5]

The size and market sway of the Company weren't the only issues. Many in Britain's upper classes had lost huge sums when the bubble burst. If Lord Liverpool's government was to have any chance of being re-elected, it needed to show it was dealing with the root causes of the crash. Thus, the VDL Co's timing could not have been worse. Bathurst and Wilmot-Horton told the VDL Co directors the government "could not therefore follow the principle granted to the Australian Company" and the Prime Minister had devised "some restrictions ... for the purpose of repressing as far as possible that Spirit of Gambling which had manifested itself so strong in the shares of other joint stock companies". These restrictions would make their stock "a most unmarketable commodity".[6]

To add insult to injury, behind the scenes MacArthur lobbied the government to make sure this new upstart monopoly in Van Diemen's Land wouldn't impinge on the profitability of *his* monopoly in New South Wales. He was concerned the scale of sheep purchases by the VDL Co would push up the price of sheep—sheep he was planning to buy. The Australian Company insisted the VDL Co be denied the right to buy any sheep directly, or indirectly, from New South Wales for a period of 12 years. Furthermore, the VDL Co should not be able to buy sheep from any European country for three years. Not surprisingly, the VDL Co directors were livid.

Bathurst played King Solomon, telling the companies to negotiate the where from and for how long restrictions, and if they couldn't agree, he'd unilaterally decide the terms. In the end, the VDL Co gained some concessions from the Australian Company, but only by reaching the outcome MacArthur wanted from the beginning. The VDL Co. could not buy sheep on the open market in New South Wales—but they could buy 5,000 from the Australian Company. In Europe, The VDL Co could only buy from Portugal or Spain, protecting MacArthur who sourced his sheep in Germany. Effectively, MacArthur got to have his lamb chop, and eat it too.

London Docks by Henry Moses, 1824.
Part two of Moses' 'Sketches of Shipping'. Reproduced with permission, Green Blackwall collection, Royal Museums Greenwich, PAD7901

Back in November 1824, James Inglis, the VDL Co managing director, had approached Edward Curr, a successful young businessman recently returned from Van Diemen's Land, to join the Company. Curr agreed and was appointed the company secretary *pro tem* (for the time being) to assist in the negotiations with the Colonial Office. But Curr was earmarked to be the man to represent the Company in Van Diemen's Land.

In 1823, Curr had sold up his interests in Hobart and sailed home to see his dying father. His father, John Curr, was a wealthy mining engineer who built the family fortune through ingenious patents mechanizing coal production. Under John Curr's patronage, the Curr family rose in society, despite being Catholic. Their home was the grand Bellevue House, just outside Sheffield. Edward and his brothers were educated at Stonyhurst College in Lancashire, the best Catholic school in England. His education complete, Curr was apprenticed to a merchant's office in Liverpool. Then at the age of 19, Curr received a sizable advance on his inheritance (£3,000 to £4,000) to enable him to seek his fortune investing in agriculture in Brazil. He spent two years there, and while Curr enjoyed life in Brazil, he decided "the laws of the country pertaining to slavery were very distasteful".[7] Curr returned to England with a better money-making plan.

On June 30, 1819, Edward Curr married Elizabeth Micklethwaite, the granddaughter of Richard Micklethwaite, 4th Lord of Ardsley. The match was eminently suitable. The Mickethwaites were also Catholic and with the marriage Curr "received a considerable amount of money".[8] Edward then took Elizabeth to Van Diemen's Land, where it appears Curr found the laws pertaining to convict labour less distasteful than slavery. They returned to England three years later when Curr learnt of his father's illness.

Unfortunately, they arrived home too late. John Curr died in January 1823, five months before they'd left Van Diemen's Land. To add to Curr's misery, the family fortune had evaporated. His father had entrusted a French priest by the name of Pére Ductiône to invest £30,000 in the French stock market and the money was lost.[9]

However, the journey was not wasted. To wile away time aboard ship, Curr wrote *An Account of the Colony of Van Diemen's Land, Principally Designed for the Use of Emigrants*[10] which espoused the merits of agricultural investment in the colony. When it was published in London in 1824, it caught the eye of the VDL Co directors.

A few months after Curr joined the company, Stephen Adey was appointed as Curr's assistant. Adey was the son of the Rev. John Adey, Clerk of Westwell in Kent. Adey worked for many years with his older brother George, running a woollen mill in Uley, Gloucestershire.[11] The Adey brothers where innovators in the cloth trade, with an 1818 article "On New Improvements in the Manufacture of superfine Woollen Cloth" noting "Mr. Adey, of Uley, has also made a considerable improvement in the machine shears."[12]

Adey was a subscriber on the Company's original petition to the Colonial Office in 1824.[13] But he desired more hands-on involvement. As soon as the Company received its Royal Charter, Adey was appointed the future "Superintendent of the Company's Lands". Curr would oversee business from Hobart, while Adey would coordinate activities out on the grant. Although the 44-year-old Adey was 17 years older than Curr, he seemed comfortable with the arrangement.

Throughout the summer of 1825, Curr and Adey worked closely, preparing for their departure to Van Diemen's Land and selecting the other "officers" who would join them in the Company's advance party, which they referred to as the "Establishment". The advertisements for the other officers appeared in the British press in July. Alexander Goldie was appointed "agriculturalist", an overblown term for the farm manager, which engendered hilarity and ridicule in the Tasmanian press.[14] John Miller was appointed "principal surveyor" but resigned within a month. Henry Hellyer was appointed "architect and surveyor" and took on Miller's role after his departure. Two junior "land surveyors" were also appointed, Joseph Fossey and Clement Lorymer.[15]

The precise location of the Company's grant was a bone of contention. The Company initially requested "the Grant of Land might be between the 147° & 148°. 20' East Longitude and 41° & 42° South Latitude".[16] This was an outrageous opening gambit—a rectangle 20 miles east-to-west and 70 miles north-to-south, centred on Launceston and encompassing much of the best pastoral land in Tasmania. The Colonial Office was sensitive to the outrage such a grant would generate. Wilmot-Horton told the directors they "were mistaken in their ideas".[17] The colonial government in Hobart had already allocated some of this land to free settlers and this gathered pace in 1824–25. The Colonial Office was determined the Company's grant be located "without inconveniencing the Colony & entrenching too closely upon private settlers".

In December 1824, Bathurst recommended the directors discuss the location of their grant with Lieutenant-Governor Sorell, who had just arrived back in England. Sorell believed the Company's grant should be in the extreme north-west, providing impetus to open up this unexplored territory.

The first 20 years of settlement in Van Diemen's Land had comfortably confined itself to the 100-mile long set of interconnected valleys stretching between Hobart and Launceston, and while the colonial population remained small, there was little need to look elsewhere. This corridor seemed like a gift from heaven. The climate was mild, the valley floors were naturally open and grassy, and the surrounding wooded hills provided ample lumber. The whole region was well-watered by rivers rising high in the mountains to the east and west.

The colonists were unaware this was an engineered landscape. Thousands of years of Aboriginal land management using fire had shaped these exquisite "parklands". In the 1820s, Sorell, and then his successor Sir George Arthur, granted more and more of this area—Tasmania's Midlands—to free settlers, and conflict was brewing. The struggle between black and white over ownership of Tasmania's pastoral resources was about to explode into what became known as the "Black War", a war into which the VDL Co would be inexorably drawn.

Recognising new pasture was becoming scarce, in late 1823 Sorell sent Charles Browne Hardwicke, a retired naval officer, and Captain John Rolland, of the 3rd Regiment, to investigate the land west of Launceston. Hardwicke performed a coastal reconnaissance and spotted grasslands near "the first Western River" (the Rubicon) as well as at Circular Head and Cape Grim in the extreme north-west. Rolland went overland and "discovered" the grasslands of the "Western Marshes" in the Chudleigh Valley. Although Hardwicke and Rolland found just a few thousand acres, Sorell was certain there was more pasture hidden in the west.

Lord Bathurst's various imprecise descriptions of the location of the VDL Co grant as the north-west "district", "part" or "quarter", led to much acrimony between Curr and the new administration of Lieutenant-Governor Arthur.[18] Curr tried to locate the grant as close as possible to Launceston, while Arthur continually thwarted him, seeking to push the Company away to Cape Grim. But this was all in the future. First, the Company's Establishment needed to get to Van Diemen's Land as quickly as possible to stake their claim.

The Company contracted a fast, new ship, the *Cape Packet*, under Captain William Kellie, to transport Curr, Adey, Hellyer, Fossey and Lorymer to Hobart. The directors consigned to Curr and Adey 20,000 Spanish dollars, equivalent to more than $1 million today. With this, they would lay the groundwork for the arrival of the Company's brig *Tranmere*, which was to follow within the year, carrying sheep, cattle, seed, equipment and indentured servants.

On September 14, 1825, the directors wished Curr and Adey well, as they "took their leave of the Court preparatory to their embarkation for Van Diemen's Land in the Ship *Cape Packet*, Captain Kellie".[19] Two days later, Kellie left the new London Docks for the port of Cowes on the Isle of Wight. At Cowes he took aboard the five VDL Co officers, Elizabeth Curr and the three Curr children, Adey's wife Lucy and her widowed sister Mary Leman Grimstone. Then followed weeks of bad weather that kept the *Cape Packet* in port. Finally, on Wednesday, October 12, 1825, she set sail for Van Diemen's Land, where in the forests and high plains of the north-west the arduous and bloody next chapter of the VDL Co would play out.

■ ■ ■

NOTES

1. Stephen H. Roberts, *History of Australian Land Settlement 1788–1920* (London: Cass & Company, 1924), 64.
2. Minutes of the Court of Directors of the Van Diemen's Land Company. National Library of Australia, Series M337-339. Vol. 1, May 12, 1824.
3. *Colonial Times and Tasmanian Advertiser*, Friday March 17, 1826, 2.
4. *The Times* (London), June 25, 1825, 2.
5. *Colonial Times and Tasmanian Advertiser*, March 17, 1826, 2.
6. Minutes of the Court of Directors, March 16, 1825.
7. Samuel Furphy, *Edward M Curr and the Tide of History* (Canberra: ANU Press, 2013), 5.
8. Edward M Curr, "Memoranda Concerning Our Family" (1877), State Library of Victoria, MS 8998.
9. Curr, "Memoranda Concerning Our Family".
10. Edward Curr, *An Account of the Colony of Van Diemen's Land, Principally Designed for the Use of Emigrants* (London George Cowie & Co., 1824).
11. *Gell & Bradshaw's Gloucestershire Directory*, 1820, 222.
12. Thomas Gill, *Annals of Philosophy* Vol. XII, July–December 1818, 213.
13. Minutes of the Court of Directors, 16 February 1825.
14. *Colonial Times and Tasmanian Advertiser*, March 17, 1826, 2.
15. Minutes of the Court of Directors, August 25, September 14, 1824.
16. Minutes of the Court of Directors, July 14, 1824.
17. Minutes of the Court of Directors, December 1, 1824.
18. Letter Books of the Van Diemen's Land Company. National Library of Australia, Series 535-358, Vol. 9, July 27, 1826.
19. Minutes of the Court of Directors, September 14, 1825.

COMMENDED, THE VAN DIEMEN HISTORY PRIZE 2022–2023

Frank Pogson Bethune

Tasmania's warrior priest

MELANIE ROYLANCE

What motivates a man of God to take up arms? Although warrior priests have existed since ancient times, in medieval Europe, canon law prohibited Christian priests from serving as soldiers, although many served on battlefields as spiritual advisors, the forerunners of modern military chaplains. Reverend Frank Pogson Bethune tended the quiet Huon parish of Ranelagh when the Great War broke out in 1914. Like many other priests, he could have helped Australia's war effort by becoming a chaplain. Instead, in June 1915, aged 38, he enlisted to fight and became one of Tasmania's most celebrated soldiers.

Bethune's story has been told and retold over the years, often blending fact with heroic myth. Official war historian Charles Bean's depiction of the Anzacs as brave and adaptable larrikin bushmen influenced Australian perceptions of their wartime experiences.[1] At face value, Bethune's courage and determination typified Bean's Anzac hero. However, Bethune was a complex man whose tenacious personality, religious principles, and beliefs in justice shaped his military experiences.

Like many officers, Bethune was born into privilege. The second son of wealthy pastoralist Walter Ross Munro Bethune and his wife, Louisa Gellibrand Pogson, he was born at Dunrobin, the family estate between Hamilton and Ouse, on April 8, 1877.[2] Dunrobin was the centre of a large estate stretching across the Midlands, started by his grandfather, Walter Angus Bethune (1794–1885), a Scottish merchant. Granted land at Hamilton in 1921, the family built a fortune over the next three decades from wheat

Captain Frank Pogson Bethune, MC,
1st Machine Gun Battalion, AIF.
Published in the Commonwealth Gazette,
*August 21, 1917; reproduced with permission of the
Australian War Memorial*

and sheep exports.[3] Considered local "gentry", along with other Midlands "shepherd king" families, they controlled large tracts of Tasmania's most productive rural land. The 1880s wool boom significantly enhanced their wealth and political power.[4] In 1903, Hobart's *The Mercury* described Hamilton as "very quiet" compared to the 1850s because land consolidation had stifled any other industry which might have benefited the township.[5]

Bethune grew up on Dunrobin with his four sisters, two brothers, and a cousin, John Bethune. Educated at the Hutchins School, Hobart, he began farming after matriculating in 1896. In 1902, after John finished school, the two young men left for England to study at Cambridge University.[6] Despite their wealth, the cousins chose to read theology at Selwyn College, a non-collegiate institution established in the 1880s as an affordable alternative to the major colleges. Focused on training future missionaries and pastors' sons, Selwyn charged low fees and encouraged simple living. The toilets were earth pits, bathing was in tin baths in the students' rooms, and lighting was by oil lamp.[7] Although not a theological college, many graduates became ordained ministers.[8]

Both men graduated with First Class Honours. Frank Bethune won a half-blue for boxing, but his academic career was not without controversy. In 1904, Selwyn suspended him for a term as punishment for setting fire to a fence during an exuberant Mafeking night celebration (the anniversary of the lifting of Mafeking's siege during the Boer War).[9]

Graduating in 1905, Bethune returned to Australia. That year, he and John were ordained as deacons in the Anglican Church, Frank at St John's, Launceston, and John at Longford.[10] In January 1907, Bethune married Laura Eileen Nicholas, from another wealthy Hamilton family, in the church at Ouse, where he had worshipped as a child. In September, he and John returned to Selwyn College to complete their Master of Arts degrees, graduating in 1908.[11] Ordained as a minister on his return to Australia, Bethune became curate at St John the Baptist Anglican Church, Hobart, and later at Sheffield, where his eldest son, Walter Angus (Premier of Tasmania from 1969–1972), was born in September 1908.[12]

Bethune moved to the Huon region in 1909 to serve as the rector at Ranelagh.[13] He and Laura added to their family with Malcolm (1910), Mary Ross (1913) and Helen Munro (1915).[14] Although under 5'7" (1.7m) and of medium build, Bethune was an active sportsperson excelling at tennis and rifle shooting. Known as "one of the best shots in the district", in 1911, he donated the Bethune Trophy for the highest scoring marksman across the year's competitions at the Franklin Rifle Club.[15]

When the Great War broke out, Bethune was in his late 30s, well-respected and busy in his parish. Yet, two months after Helen's birth, on June 30, 1915, he enlisted in the 12th Battalion, Australian Imperial Force (AIF), perhaps persuaded by the daily news reports from Gallipoli and the patriotic recruiting campaigns entreating men to replace or avenge those lost.[16] His cousin John chose not to fight, serving as a chaplain at the AIF's Claremont Training Camp, Hobart, where Frank would have been under his spiritual guidance while he underwent initial military training.[17]

Older and better educated than most enlistees, instructors soon singled out Bethune for his potential as an officer. Passing his officer's examination in August 1915, after completing 21 weeks of training, Bethune received his commission as Second Lieutenant on December 9, 1915. In February 1916, he embarked for Europe via Egypt as a reinforcement officer in the 12th Battalion.[18]

Between Alexandria and Marseilles, Bethune preached an impromptu sermon aboard the troop ship *Transylvania* carrying General Birdwood, the corps headquarters returning from Gallipoli, and 4,000 troops from the 1st Australian Division, which became widely known amongst Anzacs and the Australian public.[19] A letter from Charles Bean, published in many Australian newspapers, declared that standing beside Birdwood, Bethune "put his finger ... straight on to the heart of the nation".[20]

Revealing his motives for enlisting, Bethune referred to Germany bombing London, committing atrocities in Belgium and France, and sinking the Lusitania. He told the men they had volunteered "to say this sort of thing shall not happen in the world so long as we are in it ... We are not heroes, and we do not want to be called heroes. We should have been less than men if we hadn't ... We are on that great enterprise, with no thought of gain or conquest, but to help right a great wrong."[21] While the message of fighting injustice is clear, Bethune also alluded to the war as a test of manhood and an adventure the men would have dreamed of as boys. In this complex amalgam of motives, Bean was probably correct in saying that Bethune had captured the thoughts of the men standing before him.

Another witness to this oration was WD Evans, then Officer Commanding the troops aboard the *Transylvania,* who later selected Bethune for special training as a machine-gun commander. Like Bean, Birdwood's address and Bethune's sermon impressed Evans, who stated they "will long live in the memories of those privileged to listen".[22] Bean reported that Bethune gave the address as there was no ship's chaplain, but Evans disputed this, citing a recent burial at sea where a chaplain officiated. Evans claimed senior officers asked Bethune "because it was felt that a sermon delivered by one who was destined to share the front-line dangers and privations with those he was addressing would constitute a very strong appeal".[23]

Bethune completed training on the machine gun in France before his promotion to Lieutenant in August 1916, when assigned to the 3rd Machine Gun Company as Officer Commanding No.1 Section. As a successful leader, he enhanced his reputation for courage and duty by being awarded the Military Cross for "conspicuous gallantry and devotion to duty".[24] The recommendation stated that between February 24 and 27, before Le Barque, Bethune was "absolutely fearless", having reconnoitred no-man's-land in daylight and led his men to site their machine guns while under enemy fire. These were examples of when "his cool and courageous behaviours at all times inspired all those near him to do what would be impossible under a less intrepid leader".[25]

However, it was an action 12 months later that sealed his reputation. As the bitter winter of 1917–18 dragged on, Allied troops along the Western Front waited restlessly for an expected German assault. Like all the Australians positioned around Ypres, Belgium, Bethune knew that the Russian Revolution in October 1917 had released more than 40 German divisions from the Eastern Front. Each month, the Germans railed more and more men across Europe to bolster their weary comrades in Belgium and France. This numerical advantage might be Germany's last chance to win the war before the expected influx of more than a million American soldiers by May.[26]

At Spoil Bank, a canal levee five kilometres south of Ypres, Bethune drilled his section of seasoned men, most of who had served with him for some time.[27] Their role in any German attack was to hold their position, inflict casualties, and slow the German advance to give Australian units time to reorganise troops to strengthen the overall defence.[28] By February, fears faded that the offensive would focus on Ypres as word spread that the Germans were massing further east. Any attack through the ground torn apart in the bloody battle for Passchendaele in late 1917 was likely to be a feint to prevent the rapid redeployment of Allied troops.

When German shelling intensified in early March, the Australians moved into their prepared defensive positions. The site allocated to his fellow officer, Lieutenant JC Hoge, disheartened Bethune. In a quickly overrun death trap, the younger, less experienced officer could not bring effective fire on the enemy. Despite Bethune's vehement protests, his commanding officer refused to re-site Hoges' machine gun, so Bethune requested that he and his section man the position instead. He bluntly explained his view of the situation to his men and asked for six volunteers. His entire section stepped forward. As the chosen men moved forward, the orders changed, relocating Bethune's section to a more favourable place they were to hold "at all costs".[29] Bethune penned orders for his men, outlining what "at all costs" would mean:

Special Orders to No. 1 Section, 13/3/18
1. This position will be held, and the section will remain here until it is relieved
2. The enemy cannot be allowed to interfere with this programme
3. If the section cannot remain here alive, it will remain here dead, but in any case, it will remain here
4. Should any man through shell shock or other cause attempt to surrender, he will remain here dead

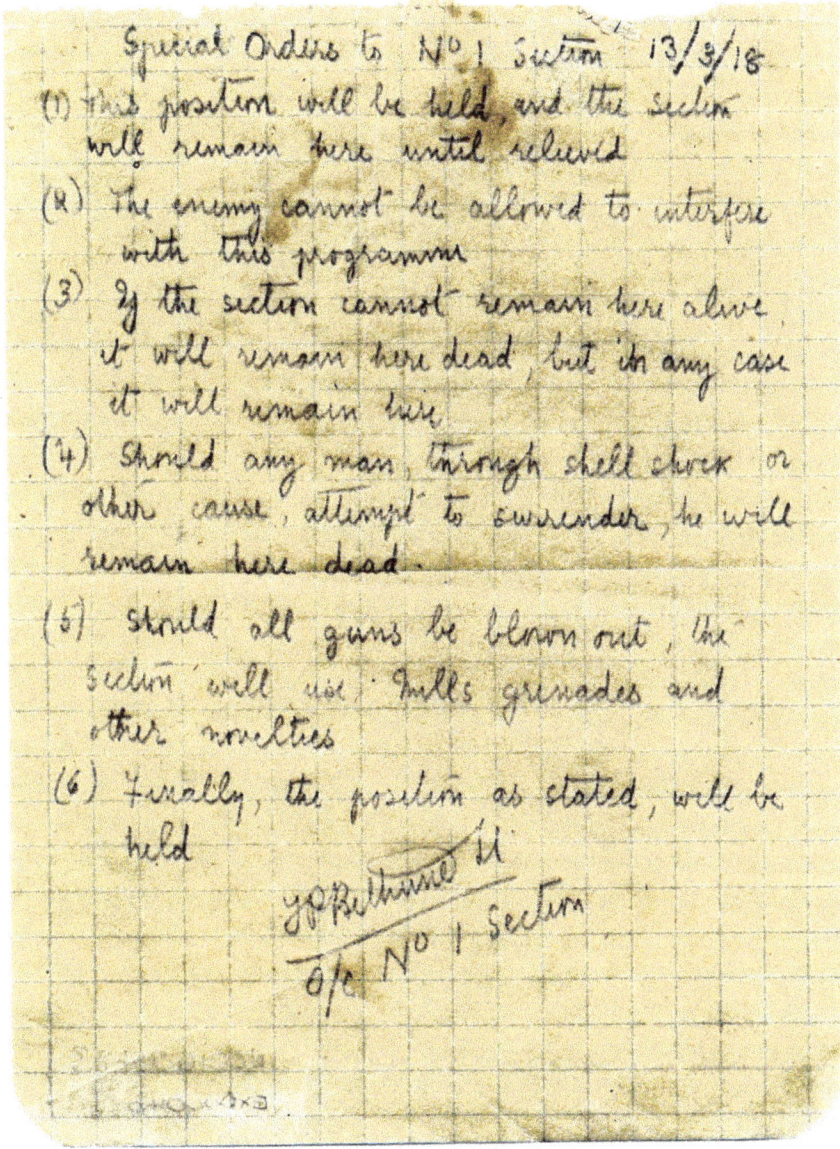

The famous order issued by Lieutenant Frank P Bethune, MC, No. 1 Section, 3rd Machine Gun Company on March 13, 1918.
Reproduced with permission of the Australian War Memorial

> 5. Should all guns be blown out, the section will use Mills grenades and other novelties
> 6. Finally, the position as stated, will be held[30]

Later known as the "do-or-die orders", Bethune's directive triggered one of the most enduring heroic myths of the war. In his *Official History*, Charles Bean retold the story and lauded Bethune's bravery and determination.[31] London's *The Times* newspaper described the orders as "inspiring and famous"—the embodiment of the sacrificial attitude of the Empire.[32] The orders soon spread across the Allied armies, with British and French commanders using them to galvanise their troops. The Americans distributed copies as "an admirable model of all that a set of standing trench orders should be".[33] After the fall of Dunkirk in June 1940, the government reproduced them on posters displayed throughout England under the caption "The spirit which won the last war".[34] Even in Australia today, the story of his orders means people remember Bethune as a "man with a strong resolve to do his duty".[35]

Many of the accounts of the orders distort the facts, however, and others conceal the circumstances and even the author's identity. Bethune's commands also attracted controversy, especially in 1933, when EGL Thurlow published *Pill-boxes of Flanders*. The preamble had a copy of the orders displayed at the Library at Talbot House, Poperinge "found in a pill-box at Passchendaele on its re-occupation" where "the Australian machine-gunners, who had occupied the position lay around dead".[36] This generated a flurry of articles and letters in British and Australian newspapers debating the orders' wording, authorship, and circumstances.

Many following this debate might have assumed from his orders that Bethune was the archetypal gung-ho young officer inspired by his duty to King and Country so often depicted in popular fiction. WA Ross DCM felt compelled to write a letter explaining that while an order to die at their posts "may seem drastic, every machine gunner knew it was their duty to hold a position at all costs … with no consideration to abandon his Vickers machine-gun … and was expected to die at his post if circumstances were grave enough to threaten the rest of the line."[37]

In August 1933, WD Evans, who a month earlier had written to correct reports of Bethune's oration on the *Transylvania*, penned an article published in the Sydney Mail defending Bethune's character against "a section of newspaper readers … so ready to accept a regrettable misinterpretation that so gravely slanders one of the finest characters that ever graced the uniform of an officer of the AIF."[38] Evans described Bethune as the opposite of "bloodthirsty", "vainglorious", and "a braggart".[39] Idolised by his men, Bethune led from the front and displayed great affection and respect for his section, never talking down to them or expounding his religious beliefs. For Evans, Bethune's action to shield Hoges from the poor machine-gun position was "a matter of unfaltering duty to a cause".[40] In issuing the orders, Bethune followed military procedures by amplifying his orders to hold the position at all costs to gain time for the main body to prepare to face the German attack.

Thurlow's book perpetuated the heroic myth of stoic death in the face of great adversity.[41] How much action the section faced is a matter of conjecture. Even the most comprehensive account of Bethune, written in 2004 on behalf of Queensland's Anzac Day Commemoration Committee, perpetuates the belief that the section faced "constant artillery barrages of high explosives, shrapnel and gas shells" over 18 days and repelled multiple attacks before being relieved. It also incorrectly implies that Bethune won his Military Cross for that action.[42] In contrast, Charles Bean's *Official History* records that they faced "nothing worse than gas shelling". In his account, Lieutenant-Colonel Milligan, a divisional staff officer who had visited Bethune's position on the day he posted the orders, shared them with the military hierarchy as an example of duty before the offensive had begun.[43]

What is certain is that the section survived intact. Bethune and his men faced the Germans in France during the initial stage of the Spring Offensive, but severe gunshot wounds in his left leg and foot cut his war short only a month after he issued the orders. Transferred to the 3rd London General Hospital at Wandsworth, he returned to France, after four months of treatment, as a temporary captain. After excelling at an officer training course, Bethune returned to his unit as captain weeks before the Armistice. As the winter of 1918 set in, his wounds played up, and he returned to London, where doctors had to amputate most of his big toe.[44]

Bethune returned to Tasmania in May 1919 but never recovered fully from the war. In 1921, he claimed against the Repatriation Department for failing health because of breathing problems resulting from gas attacks at Passchendaele. They denied it as his official record showed no exposure to gas. By then, Bethune had returned to Cluny, one of the family estates near Ouse. He farmed there until 1936, when he retired to Hobart and became a keen golfer.[45]

After the war, Bethune never returned to religious life but periodically assisted the Hamilton parish, especially in services to commemorate the Anzacs. In 1929, he "delivered a most feeling address" at the funeral of Arthur Jenkins, a man from Ouse who succumbed to his war injuries a decade after hostilities ended.[46]

Bethune died of cerebrovascular disease in Hobart on December 4, 1942, aged 65.[47] Syndicated throughout Australia and Britain, Bethune's obituaries revived memories of his orders and his sermon on the *Transylvania*, still framing both as heroic willingness to sacrifice personal safety to defend others.[48]

Bethune never responded to the 1933 debate about his orders or his motives. Recently, some historians have critiqued the Anzac mythology and Australia's participation in the war as zealous imperial patriotism.[49] While this may be true, we can only judge people's actions through their contemporary understanding of events. So, what motivated Bethune? Based on the citation for his Military Cross, he arguably had a reckless disregard for his safety. Postcards from the Western Front sent to his young son Angus described events like a boy's own adventure, especially after significant battles. However, as Angus was only a child, Bethune likely catered to the lad's understanding of war and concern for his father.[50]

Commentators treating Bethune as a severe man for whom fairness and duty to King, Country and his fellow man were paramount, omit to look at him as a man with a young family, a sportsman, and a priest who had been popular in his parish. Was his exuberant fence-burning on Mafeking Night more reflective of a man of patriotic duty, or did it reveal a high-spirited man with a sense of adventure? It was probably both. Bethune was not a dour zealot but a popular leader of his men. Annoyed with the attitude of his commanding officer, Bethune wrote and displayed the orders to make a point that, as volunteers, he and his section did not need reminding about their duty. As quoted by John Laffin, Bethune's correspondence about how his section understood his orders not to surrender confirms that "they knew that I knew they could not seriously consider such a possibility and so between us, we enjoyed in silence the joke that to an outsider might have seemed a little grim".[51]

Perhaps the best explanation for Bethune becoming a warrior priest is contained in his *Transylvania* sermon, where he portrayed the war as primarily a moral duty to defend the oppressed in the cause of freedom mixed with the human desire for adventure and the opportunity to test one's mettle.

■ ■ ■

NOTES

1. Helen Robinson, "Lest We Forget? The Fading of New Zealand War Commemorations, 1946–1966," *New Zealand Journal of History* 44, no. 1 (2010): 76-9; DA Kent, "The Anzac Book and the Anzac Legend: C. E. W. Bean as Editor and Image-maker," *Australian Historical Studies* 21, no. 84 (1985): 377–8; and Joan Beaumont, "ANZAC Day to VP Day: Arguments and Interpretations," *Journal of the Australian War Memorial* 40 (February 2007) https://www.awm.gov.au/articles/journal/j40/beaumont.
2. Tasmanian Birth Certificate, District of Hamilton, 118/1877, Frank Pogson Bethune; and Peter Chapman, "Bethune, Frank Pogson (1877–1942)", *Australian Dictionary of Biography*, Australian National University, accessed March 18, 2021, https://adb.anu.edu.au/biography/bethune-frank-pogson-5226/text8795.
3. Peter Chapman, "Bethune, Walter Angus (1794–1885)", *Australian Dictionary of Biography*, Australian National University, accessed March 18, 2021, https://adb.anu.edu.au/biography/bethune-walter-angus-1775/text1991.
4. Henry Reynolds, "'Men of Substance and Deservedly Good Repute': The Tasmanian Gentry 1856–1875", *Australian Journal of Politics and History* 15 (December 1969): 61–4, 68; and Helen Moyle, *Australia's Fertility Transition: A Study of 19th Century Tasmania* (Canberra: ANU Press, 2020), 44.
5. "Hamilton", *The Mercury*, August 31, 1903, 6.
6. Chapman, "Bethune, Frank Pogson".
7. The Master, Fellow and Scholars Selwyn College, Cambridge, *Selwyn College 1882–1973 A Short History*, (Cambridge: Selwyn, 1973), accessed August 16, 2022, https://www.sel.cam.ac.uk/about/selwyn-history.
8. Ibid.
9. Chapman, "Bethune, Frank Pogson".
10. "The Gazette", *The Mercury*, December 12, 1905, 7.
11. Tasmanian Marriage Certificate, District of Hamilton, 209/1907, Frank Pogson Bethune and Laura Eileen Nicholas; and "University Herald, Cambridge", *The Cambridge Independent Press*, October 30, 1908, 8.
12. Chapman, "Bethune, Frank Pogson"; and Parliament of Tasmania, "History Resources—Members of Parliament, Walter Angus Bethune," accessed August 14, 2022, https://www.parliament.tas.gov.au/history/members/bethunew480.html.
13. "Rev. F. P. Bethune Enlists", *Huon Times*, June 9, 1915, 5.
14. Tasmanian Birth Certificate, District of Victoria (Huon), 4161/1910, Malcolm Bethune, Tasmanian Birth Certificate, District of Victoria (Huon), 5615/1913, Mary Rose Bethune, and Tasmanian Birth Certificate, District of Victoria(Huon), 4430/1915, Helen Munro Bethune.
15. Service Record Frank Pogson Bethune; "Rev. F. P. Bethune Enlists," 5; and "Rifle Shooting", *Huon Times*, August 19, 1911, 2.
16. Service Record Frank Pogson Bethune.
17. Chapman, "Bethune, Frank Pogson".
18. Service Record Frank Pogson Bethune.
19. WD Evans, "Letters: War Epic", *Sydney Morning Herald*, July 12, 1933, 6.

20. CEW Bean, *Letters from France* (London: Cassell and Company, 1917), 6.
21. Ibid, 4–6.
22. Evans, "Letters: War Epic", 6.
23. Bean, Letters from France, 3; and Ibid.
24. Service Record Frank Pogson Bethune.
25. "Recommendation for Honours and Awards," Australian War Memorial, accessed August 14, 2022, https://s3-ap-southeast-2.amazonaws.com/awm-media/collection/RCDIG1068728/document/5514479.PDF.
26. John Hussey, "The Movement of German Divisions to the Western Front, Winter 1917–1918," *War in History* 4 No. 2, (April 1997): 213–220.
27. WD Evans, "A War Epic of Flanders," *Sydney Mail*, August 2, 1933, 16.
28. Ibid.
29. CEW Bean, *Official History of Australia in the War of 1914–1918, Volume V—The Australian Imperial Force in France during the Main German Offensive, 1918* (8th ed., Sydney: Angus and Robertson,1941): 110.
30. Ibid.
31. Ibid.
32. Chapman, "Bethune, Frank Pogson".
33. Quoted in John Laffin, *Australians at War: The Western Front 1917–18*, (Sydney: Time-Life, 1988), 69.
34. Chapman, "Bethune, Frank Pogson".
35. Bethune was the subject of the oration at the 2021 Nambour Anzac Day Service in Queensland. "Clergyman's stirring words inspired remarkable Anzac courage under fire", *Sunshine Valley Gazette,* accessed August 14, 2022, https://www.sunshinevalleygazette.com.au/blog/nambour-anzac-day-2021.
36. Col. EGL Thurlow, *The Pill-boxes of Flanders*, (London: Ivor Nicholson and Watson 1933), i.
37. WA Ross, "Correspondence: Pill-Boxes of Flanders", *Kalgoorlie Miner*, July 22, 1933, 2.
38. Evans, 'A War Epic of Flanders', 16.
39. Ibid.
40. Ibid.
41. "War Epic: Story of Australian Heroism," *Sydney Morning Herald*, July 10, 1933, 9.
42. Darryl Kelly, *Just Soldiers: Stories of Ordinary Australians Doing Extraordinary Things in Time of War*, (Brisbane: ANZAC Day Commemoration Committee, 2004), 4–8.
43. Bean, *Official History of Australia in the War of 1914–1918, Volume V*, 110.
44. Service Record Frank Pogson Bethune.
45. "Obituary Capt. F. P. Bethune, Author of Epic Order In First World War", *The Mercury*, December 5, 1942, 7.
46. "Death From War Wounds", *The Mercury*, December 31, 1929, 6.
47. "Obituary Capt. F. P. Bethune", 7.
48. For example, "Parson who gave 'Hold On' Order", *Manchester Evening News*, December 23, 1942, 4; "Wrote Famous Passchendaele Order", *Dundee Evening Telegraph*, December 23, 1942, 2; and "This Position Will Be Held", *Halifax Evening Courier*, December 23, 1942, 3.

49. For example, Marilyn Lake and Henry Reynolds (eds), *What's Wrong with Anzac? The Militarisation of Australian History*, (Sydney: NewSouth, 2010).
50. Tasmanian Museum and Art Gallery, "Postcards of Frank Pogson Bethune," *First World War Exhibition*, accessed September 23, 2021, https://ww1exhibition.tmag.tas.gov.au/__data/assets/pdf_file/0014/191021/Bethune-Postcards.pdf; and Scott Bennett and Barbara Bennett, *Biographical Register of the Tasmanian Parliament 1825–1980*, (Hobart: Parliament of Tasmania, 2016), p. 25.
51. Laffin, *Australians at War*, 69.

COMMENDED, THE VAN DIEMEN HISTORY PRIZE 2022-2023

Gold amongst the tin

RAY BASSETT

My affection for the West Coast of Tasmania began as a boy in the '70s when my family started visiting a shack near Granville Harbour. In those days I was more interested in the fishing and exploring than the history of the place. At first glance, it didn't look like it had much of a history. I did find it surprising that there could have been 300 men clambering over that rock looking for a tin bonanza, but I didn't doubt it. On the epic journey (for us kids) from Wynyard, we would get to hear the stories, we'd visit the museum in Zeehan, and then we'd see the evidence.

In those days, the track left Zeehan for Trial Harbour along the south of the range, then turned north along Climies Track across the tableland between the mountain and the Great Southern Ocean. There were plenty of holes in the hills, rotting structures and rusting remains to be seen in those days that we were never allowed to explore.

Later, in my teens, the Hydro[1] was getting stuck into damming the Pieman River, and built a road from Zeehan to the worksite. We still had to drive to Zeehan, but now we could travel along the northern side of the mountain, and on a better dirt road, dramatically shortening the stage from Zeehan to the coast. When the Pieman works were completed, the road was sealed and connected through to the Murchison Highway north of Tullah, bypassing all the populated centres that used to mark our progress in the past. I was living in Melbourne by this stage, and while I did miss the journey as it was in the old days, in practical terms the new route was much quicker. I was making the odd visit from the mainland, occasionally taking friends down to see my "Wild West".

A view over the shacks at Big Rocky, looking toward the northern flank of Mount Heemskirk. From the early seventies, I was a regular visitor to Big Rocky and fell in love with this wild, remote spot.
Ray Bassett

I had also developed an interest in history, a resource that came to the fore when I formed a musical duo with another Tasmanian in the new millennium, writing, singing and performing story songs charactered from our own experiences or those of history. Always Australian stories. Or better, Tasmanian. We still play occasionally in Victoria's gold fields region.

Things were going swimmingly until a light bulb moment in 2012 turned everything upside down. In the roiling furnace of that imaginative fission there formed an idea that was bigger than anything I had previously conceived, and the West Coast was front and centre.

It would be a further year before I had a plan, but well before then I had come to the realisation that it was going to be something of a big job. I didn't know near enough about Mount Heemskirk, not even after re-reading everything I had—Blainey, Binks, Howard *et al*. My problem was that the period I wanted to investigate most seemed to be the least documented.

The actual details of the years surrounding the Mount Heemskirk tin boom were thin on the ground, and all the books I had read on the subject contained the same information, presented in much the same manner—a few

The primary reason for any visit to Big Rocky was to go fishing, and that was indeed the case when this photo was taken in 1991 at the mouth of the creek. An interest in the history of Mount Heemskirk wouldn't develop until much later.
Ray Bassett

good yarns, some data and disconnected events, but little to form a picture of the character of the day to day. This bottleneck in the historical narrative was the spur that provided the motivation to find a way to get behind that single account and expose the ideas, events and identities that shaped the boom.

The internet is a wonderful thing, mostly, and so I started browsing, collecting and collating. I soon discovered Trove, and it is from that wonderful resource that the great bulk of my information has been drawn.

My first "discovery" was the series of articles from which my history books had drawn their information. Printed in the *Zeehan and Dundas Herald* between November 21 and December 25, 1896, the series of six articles entitled West Coast History reflects on the events leading up to Zeehan's silver boom. It is currently the definitive story of the Heemskirk boom.

Now I had my starting point, and a rough idea of how to unravel it. Digging deeper, I soon had the opposite problem to that which I had started with. I was amassing a plethora of information, of which most was irrelevant, and all of it confusing. I had severely underestimated the task. To make sense of any of it, I was going to have to read, and keep reading; to map it all out, make it understandable. It became, and still is, a go-to activity in my idle moments.

My other process for getting behind the 1896 articles was to begin taking it apart one bite at a time. Pick a choice nibble, and start chewing.

To test the method, I chose an obvious contender, for me, to open my campaign. It is the tale of "Black Bella", a story connected with the early days of the boom. It is only a couple of paragraphs long, but in tone it has "Wild West" stamped all over it.

The tale concerns the repercussions after a man named Messiah stabs and wounds a woman named Black Bella in a fit of jealousy. Not much is said of Messiah and we are told that Black Bella is only the second woman to visit the place. She is popular with the young miners, according to the tale, and in the outrage that followed Messiah's attack, and having no lawman on hand, the miners held a kangaroo court, miner EJ Peever acting as judge. Messiah was convicted, banished from the West Coast, and given a half hour head start before a pursuit would be mounted. Messiah's aim was to make it over the Pieman River before being caught—and strung up. He wasn't caught, but it is difficult to know if the men would have gone through with their threat if they had.[2]

This story, like many in the articles describing this period, is undated and vague. Who was Messiah? Who was Black Bella? What caused the stabbing? When did this happen? I was curious and, for my intended project, I needed to know.

To my surprise, Messiah proved easy to find, due to the footprint of his shady activity while in Tasmania. Black Bella was more difficult, but enough emerged to make an informed guess. There is no direct evidence to confirm the kangaroo court, but there is a tantalising aside made by a correspondent referring to reports on Messiah's time on the West Coast, to the effect that if true he "had cleared to get out of the jurisdiction of Judge Lynch".[3]

There was more than enough to say that the tale was probably true. I had a handle on the participants, and I had narrowed the time frame for the incident to the last few months of 1881. The last piece of the jigsaw, the why of it all, would remain elusive for a little longer. For a while I thought I had perhaps found all that there was available in the digital records on the matter.

At the time of the stabbing, Trial Harbour and the hamlet that would become Remine had been in existence for 10 months. There was an air of excitement and optimism about the place, the talk of Mount Heemskirk rivalling Mount Bischoff was being fuelled by the money and plans being brought to bear at the leading claims. As Christmas 1881 and the holidays approached, those miners who are staying at Mount Heemskirk were buoyed by the arrival of a consignment of wine, spirits and beer aboard the steam vessel Amy for the opening of John Conrad's public house in Trial Harbour on New Year's Day.[4] Messiah and Black Bella were among them.

Albert Frederick Augustus Plantagenet Messiah[5] had arrived in Launceston from London in January of 1881 aboard the barque Araunah, on which he was employed as a cook. On March 8, 1881, he was charged with absenting himself from the ship without leave and given a six-week gaol term, with hard labour.[6] Within weeks of his release he was back in a Launceston court, called to give evidence in a mine salting case.[7] He was still in Tasmania in September and on his way to the West Coast, according to a report from a visiting New Zealand prospector.[8]

It is from this account that something of the man is revealed, although he mistakes Messiah's first name. The author and his party shared a night at the Mount Cleveland hut with several other parties on their walk from Waratah to Mount Heemskirk. Messiah is one of the 13 men holed up in the 16 feet by 12 feet, three-bunk hut. It is revealed that Messiah had variously been a missionary in Africa and the West Indies, a reporter and correspondent, a lawyer's clerk, a ship's cook, and a charcoal burner at Mount Bischoff. He is described only as a coloured gentlemen, rather fond of his own name, and a fine cook. The author reports that Messiah was seen some time later working as a charcoal burner at Mount Heemskirk.

His next appearance was after the incident with Black Bella. Having quit the West Coast Messiah was apprehended and charged with fraud in Hobart. It appears that Messiah had been passing off scrip in a fictious West Coast claim called the Scottish Chieftain and enjoying himself on the proceeds, then signed on with Burton's Circus as a "bounding Ethiopian of the desert", and was about to leave town. Perhaps feeling the heat, Messiah ran away from the circus and shipped onboard the Wagoola as a cook,[9] but concerned shareholders in the Scottish Chieftain got wind of it and he was arrested before the ship could depart for London.[10] Messiah managed to confuse the court proceedings and one charge was dropped, but the magistrates, on the balance of evidence of his inconsistent behaviour, convicted Messiah and sentenced him to 12 months hard labour.[11]

Black Bella proved to be much more elusive. Being a poor black woman in late colonial Tasmania, Bella would have had to make the best of whatever hand she was dealt, which wouldn't have been much. Her name may be the title of the tale, but the story is about Messiah. Bella is almost invisible, but not quite. Eventually a candidate in the person of Isabella Donnelly emerged. It is impossible to be certain, but a court report from 1882 mentions an Isabella Donnelly, alias James, alias Black Bella.[12] A further report from 1884 mentions Isabella James, alias Harbottle (Harbuckle?), alias Black Bella,[13] and another report on the same incident confirms her dark skin.[14] She was arrested for stabbing her paramour in Latrobe. Black Bella appears in a number of other reports over the years leading away from the stabbing, always for low level crime, vagrancy, disorderly conduct, et al. It is interesting to note that one of the later records details the arrest of Bella Harbuckle (possibly Black Bella) in 1890 for a stabbing incident at the Silver King Hotel in Remine, Trial Harbour.[15]

I now had a handle on the main actor and his possible victim. Messiah was definitely in Trial Harbour between mid-September 1881 and mid-January 1882, and although I could not definitively place my Black Bella at the scene, I felt that the reports I had found made it a distinct possibility. How many Black Bellas were there in Tasmania at the time?

This information, and the aside to "Judge Lynch", was enough to convince me that the tale of Messiah and Black Bella was substantially true. The result had also proved my theory of targeting specific incidents to be a worthwhile tool.

Meanwhile, the discipline of structured reading, noting and collating of the mass of information was about to prove its worth, and provide the breakthrough. As I learnt more, I began to make connections between seemingly unrelated accounts. Aspects of the information I had absorbed were beginning to resonate as I slowly plied my way through the minutiae of day to day events during the period.

Then, one moment I was reading about some local disturbance, in the next I had the last piece of the puzzle. In fact, I had several when I realised that seemingly unconnected articles were all talking, in a roundabout way, about the same precipitating incident that led to Messiah making his cameo in the annals of West Coast folklore.

The breakthrough came when reading a short letter to the editor complaining of the lack of foresight of issuing licences for two public houses in Trial Harbour without any constabulary. It went on to describe a disturbance connected with the pub, and by the time I got to the "disgraceful scenes that took place with a black women openly"[16] I began to feel like I had hit the jackpot.

The writer, On Looker, describes scenes of wild debauchery after the men couldn't wait for opening day and raided Conrad's pub, carrying off the booze and having an alcohol-fuelled bender on the beach. The writer implies that the rush on the pub may have been more a concerted plan than impulse, and that Conrad's resistance appeared little more than to make show. Scarcely a man did not sport a black eye or broken nose, such was the fighting, and several inebriates had to be rescued from the surf. The writer describes it as pandemonium, and repeated on Sundays (pay day) now that the pub was open.

I soon found a confirming editorial which mentioned an attempted stabbing[17] and acts of larrikinism that went unpunished. Retracing my steps, I found an article in which *The Mercury* correspondent reports a quiet Christmas at Mount Heemskirk, specifically mentioning the absence of drunken revelry, and is dated December 29.[18] The writer also questions the wisdom of granting two liquor licences without a resident constable or the accoutrements of law enforcement. On the face of it, the incident involving Messiah and Black Bella could have occurred within the week or so following the 29th, but my money is on December 30 or New Year's Eve.

And there it was. At the close of 1881 there'd been a raid on the pub at Trial Harbour, a drunken riot involving a stabbing, and a kangaroo court dispensing frontier justice. How Wild West is that?

That the full story was never completely expounded upon at the time perhaps reflects a certain tact on the part of the press. The government was harangued for its oversight nevertheless, which they would promptly compound with a classic knee jerk reaction, but in general terms, reports of civil unrest, and a stabbing to boot, on the nascent tin field were not good for business, let alone the possibility of collateral legal action if it were widely reported. The story of Messiah and Black Bella would only be told in print at the safe remove of some 15 years, and even then, there is no mention of the general state of affairs at Trial Harbour that resulted in the kangaroo court.

The picture is by no means complete. How old were they? Where were they from? Missing data notwithstanding, the new information has given the tale some context within the historical framework of West Coast history, and that was the aim. To find the tributary narratives that come together to become the tale, or not, as the case may be.

There are many gaps in our understanding of the motivations, actions and personalities that drove the quest for another Mount Bischoff, shaping the pioneering history of the West Coast and laying the foundation for the later Zeehan discoveries. Perhaps, in finding the information to substantiate the story of Black Bella, a small gap has been narrowed.

■ ■ ■

NOTES

1. Hydro-Electric Commission of Tasmania.
2. "West Coast History", *Zeehan and Dundas Herald* (Tas.: 1890–1922), December 25, 1896, 1 (supplement to the *Zeehan & Dundas Herald*); accessed September 3, 2022 <http://nla.gov.au/nla.news-article84538775>.
3. "Our Hobart Letter", *Launceston Examiner* (Tas.: 1842–1899) February 10, 1882: 2; accessed September 3, 2022 <http://nla.gov.au/nla.news-article38267396>.
4. "Mining", *The Mercury* (Hobart, Tas.: 1860–1954), December 12, 1881, 3; accessed September 4, 2022 <http://nla.gov.au/nla.news-article9003445>.
5. "A Prospector's Notes in Tasmania", *Launceston Examiner* (Tas.: 1842–1899) November 19, 1881, 1 (supplement to the *Launceston Examiner*); accessed September 4, 2022 <http://nla.gov.au/nla.news-article38228532>.
6. "Launceston Police Court", *Launceston Examiner* (Tas.: 1842–1899), March 9, 1881, 1 (supplement to the *Launceston Examiner*); accessed September 4, 2022 <http://nla.gov.au/nla.news-article38220250>.
7. "Police Court", *The Tasmanian* (Launceston, Tas.: 1881–1895), May 7, 1881, 429; accessed September 4, 2022 <http://nla.gov.au/nla.news-article199522839>.
8. "A Prospector's Notes in Tasmania", *Launceston Examiner* (Tas.: 1842–1899), November 19, 1881, 1 (supplement to the *Launceston Examiner*); accessed September 4, 2022 <http://nla.gov.au/nla.news-article38228532>.
9. "The Mercury", *The Mercury*, (Hobart, Tas.: 1860–1954) January 28, 1882, 2; accessed September 4, 2022 <http://nla.gov.au/nla.news-article218199511>.
10. "A Sable Scrip Seller", *Telegraph* (Launceston, Tas.: 1881–1883), February 1, 1882, 2; accessed 4 September 4, 2022 <http://nla.gov.au/nla.news-article218199511>.
11. "Our Hobart Letter", *The Tasmanian* (Launceston, Tas.: 1881–1895), February 11, 1882, 17; accessed 4 September 4, 2022 <http://nla.gov.au/nla.news-article201185789>.
12. "Hobart Police Court", *Launceston Examiner* (Tas.: 1842–1899) 3 June 1882, 3; accessed September 4, 2022 <http://nla.gov.au/nla.news-article38271546>.
13. "The Mercury", *The Mercury* (Hobart, Tas.: 1860–1954) June 13, 1884, 2; accessed September 4, 2022 <http://nla.gov.au/nla.news-article9019406>.
14. "Tasmanian Telegrams", *The Mercury* (Hobart, Tas.: 1860–1954) June 7, 1884, 3; accessed September 5, 2022 <http://nla.gov.au/nla.news-article9026175>.
15. "Country News", *The Mercury* (Hobart, Tas.: 1860–1954) February 8, 1890, 1 (*The Mercury* supplement); accessed September 4, 2022 <http://nla.gov.au/nla.news-article9228566>.
16. "Heemskirk As It Is", *The Mercury* (Hobart, Tas.: 1860–1954) January 21, 1882, 2 (*The Mercury* supplement); accessed September 5, 2022 <http://nla.gov.au/nla.news-article9004980>.
17. "The Mercury", *The Mercury* (Hobart, Tas.: 1860–1954) February 15, 1882, 2; web: September 5, 2022 <http://nla.gov.au/nla.news-article9005917>.
18. "Mount Heemskirk", *The Mercury* (Hobart, Tas.: 1860–1954) January 13, 1882, 3; accessed September 5, 2022 <http://nla.gov.au/nla.news-article9004634>.

Mysterious broken binding proves a silver lining

CARLA BAKER

The broken binding found in the first volume of Mrs W Fletcher's set of three music folios from 1834 provides a tantalising mystery. When being prepared for sale by Melbourne-based antiquarian Douglas Stewart, the broken binding revealed a newspaper scrap from Tasmania in 1833. Following this Tasmanian connection, the Allport Library and Museum of Fine Arts in Hobart acquired these historical treasures. These music folios contain so much more than exquisitely decorated music. They reveal a glimpse of life in Hobart Town earlier than what is currently available. At the time of writing, there are no other Tasmanian music folios owned by women from this period held within the Tasmanian archives.

Mrs Fletcher's music folios allow us to break down the obsession with unmarried women and domestic music to provide insight into how music was equally relevant to a married woman and her family. They also allow her voice to be heard where previously it had been drowned out by the highly-documented patriarchal establishment. Archival work such as this contributes to recalibrating the balance between the more dominant mainstream and those who are marginalised.[1]

Mrs William Fletcher, née Hannah Hone, arrived in Hobart in 1824 as the teenage daughter of Joseph Hone, the first Master of the Supreme Court for Van Diemen's Land.[2] She cemented her place within the Hobart Town aristocracy with her marriage in 1826 to William Fletcher, a well-travelled officer who was posted within the Commissariat Department in Hobart Town.[3] The

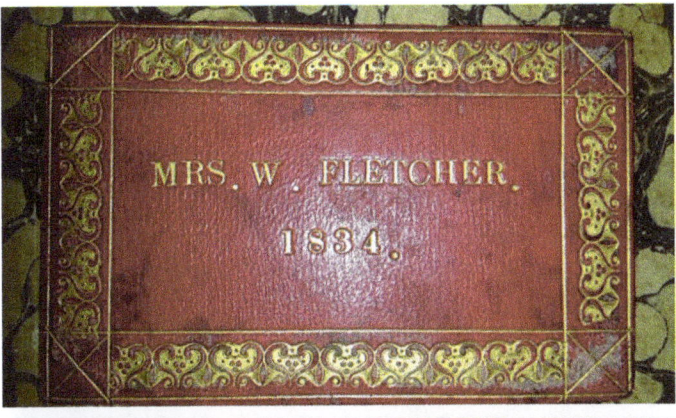

Nameplate and spine of one of Mrs W Fletcher's three matching music folios.[4]
Carla Baker

superiority of Hannah's folios befits their situation in one of the most powerful and privileged families in Van Diemen's Land at the time.[5]

Each of Hannah's folios was bound with a matching elegance, featuring a gold gilt finish on the labels, borders and spine, beautifully set off by red leather and marbled boards. This sophisticated binding was typical of music folios, requiring specialised tools and stationery to compile. Collections of elaborately bound sheet music provided a physical exhibition of wealth coveted by the settlers in Hobart Town. This heady combination of money and culture provided the influx of free settlers who were jostling for social position confirmation of membership within the colonial elite.

The growth of sheet music sales in Hobart Town from 1824–1834 followed British trends that worshipped the pianoforte and sheet music within

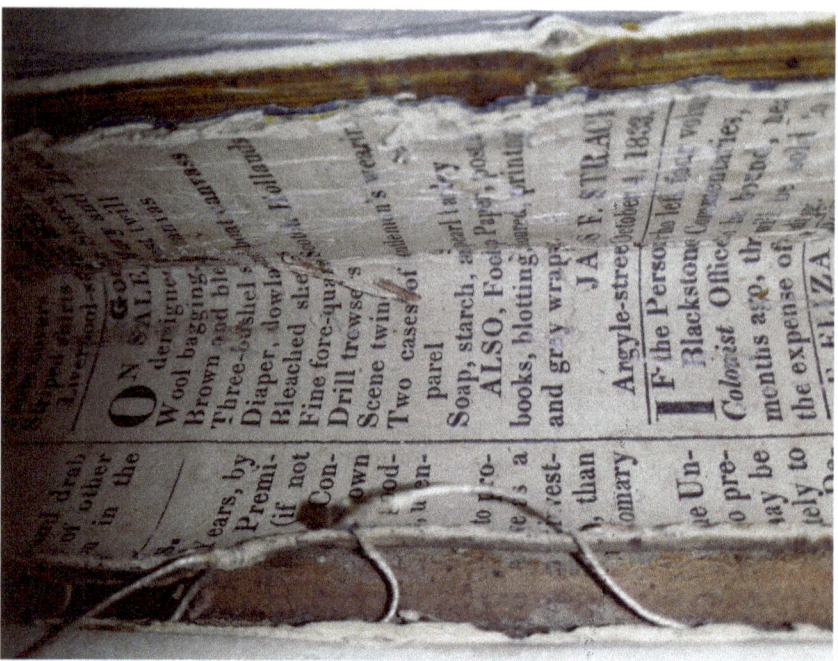

Newspaper fragment found within the broken binding.[6]
Carla Baker

the domestic space. As sheet music was readily available in Hobart Town from 1824, it's no surprise that by the time Hannah's folios were bound in 1834 there were numerous binders capable of this.

No binder label was attached to any of Hannah's folios to show the binder's identity. However, we can use the clues available within the folios to deduce feasible options. Firstly, Trove can help pinpoint the exact publication in which the advertisement in the broken binding is featured. Even though October 4, 1833, is clearly visible, that doesn't confirm the publication date.

This advertisement appeared several times in various publications, with the folio scrap appearing in the *Colonist and Van Diemen's Land Commercial and Agricultural Advertiser* on November 5, 1833. This suggests the creation of these folios was late 1833 or early 1834. In 1833–34, there were four men in Hobart Town who had access to binding equipment and stationery: George Peck, James Wood, Andrew Bent and Dr James Ross.

The National Bibliographic Database archival entry for these folios lists George Henry Peck as the likely binder as he arrived in Hobart Town in June 1833 with his "newly erected shop" launched on January 28, 1834.[7] It could be argued that he gifted these folios to Hannah to engage her as a 19th-century version of a social influencer. Even though Peck does appear a promising option, I contend other binders have a higher likelihood of being responsible for the creation of Hannah's folios. Peck appears to consider his binder trade as a supplement to his musical career. His initial focus on public performance, appearing as early as July 5, 1833, demonstrates his primary interest in building his reputation in music.[8]

James Wood was clerk of the Supreme Court upon his arrival in 1829 but resigned in September 1830.[9] This was presumably to work solely on bookbinding and sales with his wife; their shop was opened in 1829.[10] Hannah may have recognised his name in connection with her father, however Wood appears to promote lithographic illustrations as opposed to elegant book bindings, according to advertisements in October 1833.[11]

Andrew Bent was a well-known printer and publisher in Hobart, advertising his stock of "ornamental tools and assortment of coloured leathers" in 1832.[12] However, his efforts are also generally acknowledged to have been focused on antagonising the colonial establishment, as he was jailed for libel.[13] He was also an ex-convict, arriving in Hobart in 1812.[14] Bent's notoriety sullied his relationship with the colonial elite, such as Hannah.

I believe the most likely binder of Hannah Fletcher's folios to be Dr James Ross. He had a long association with government printing and the binding of speciality documents.[15] Therefore, he would have had access to appropriate materials and was "one of the best-known literary men in Hobart Town".[16] In 1834, he held the monopoly on government printing, as he had done since 1828.[17] This provides a strong link to the Commissariat Department and therefore William Fletcher, Hannah's husband. Ross and Joseph Hone, Hannah's father, were also closely connected. Ross featured an engraving of Hone's residence at the front of his 1830 *Hobart Town Almanack*.[18] They were also both prominent members of the Van Diemen's Land Mechanics' Institute.[19]

Ross' printing monopoly was challenged in 1833 when tenders were put out for "letter press, copper plate printing and book binding",[20] but the tender was won by Ross, who continued as the sole government printer until 1836.[21] Furthermore, the paper fragment found in the broken binding was from one of Andrew Bent's papers. As he was Ross' main rival, it would be poetic to think Ross was symbolically getting back at Bent by utilising his prized publication in a scrap paper form. I like to think that these folios were a gift from Dr James Ross to William Fletcher to thank him for his ongoing support and awarding the printing tender in his favour.

Sheet music in Van Diemen's Land holds the potential to articulate colonial power by monumentalising domesticity. Hannah and her music are placed in a "pivotal position at the intersection of state and nation, of public and private ... as intimate yet excluded citizens they shaped the meaning and value of the state".[22] As Hannah transitioned from an unmarried woman to a wife and mother, her music also moved from an unbound state to bound within a folio as part of a collection. Just as Hannah's sheet music was bound into a folio, she also became bound to a collection of people as wife and mother. These insights disrupt the persistent cultural ideologies around sheet music being important only to accomplished unmarried women.

The domestic idyll of the private sphere within the home was promoted as a way to provide order. Women were tasked to be the upholders of moral order, providing respite for husbands within the home from the chaotic external world by being "good" themselves.[23] The domestic woman was the keeper of this space and "was shaped to her destiny as sweet preserver and comforter, the vessel and safeguard of tradition".[24] To achieve this, women needed sophisticated social skills and lofty literary, musical and artistic culture in order to be seen as successful wives.[25] This was obtained through demonstration of the acquisition of accomplishments, particularly music.

Colonial domesticity was an explicitly gendered space, placing women at the centre of the imperial project. When domesticity is used as a category of analysis, there is no isolating the domestic from empire.[26] Hannah and her family were early colonisers in Van Diemen's Land and therefore would have felt an urgent need to rectify the lack of civilisation perceived within the penal colony. The establishment of their home would have been significant as this symbolised the arrival of modernity and civilization, a principal symbol of colonial dominance.[27] Additionally, their elevated position within elite domesticity reinforced their duty and responsibility to promote the political and public order within their own home. As a young colonial wife trying to play her part within society, Hannah's "successful home was to be seen as a contribution to empire".[28]

As the home represented a microcosm of the colony, particular household items, such as music, can be viewed as intimately entwined with colonial expansion. The collection and binding of Hannah's music into folios is a physical manifestation of the importance of consumption practice to 19th-century culture.[29] Female collectors, like Hannah, are relatively absent from formal collecting records and Hannah's folios contribute to breaking down the "privileging of masculine collecting styles".[30] Collecting music was associated with the formation of a cultured, cultivated taste by evoking aristocratic connotations. Accumulating a sheet music collection was considered a virtuous interest for a married woman as it showcased her husband's reputation, as well as providing comfort and benefit for family and visitors. Instead of solely being used as musical entertainment, the spectacle of bound music folios situated within a library implied an atmosphere of gentility and civility to guests.

Hannah's music folios provided a vehicle to convey her idealised visions of domestic life for external consumption.[31] Her carefully selected decorative binding choices and pieces of music contained within reflect her awareness of how best to convey her membership of elite society. Hannah was not only declaring her sophisticated taste but utilising music as a silver lining, to preserve her concept of security and civilisation whilst coming of age in Van Diemen's Land.

■ ■ ■

NOTES

1. Sirpa Salenius, 'On Archival Research: Recovering and Rewriting History. The Case of Sarah Parker Remond', *Transatlantica* 1 (2021), 2.
2. Lieut.-Governor Arthur to Earl Bathurst (Despatch No.10), October 20, 1824, *Historical Records of Australia Series III. Despatches and Papers relating to the settlement of the States: Volume IV Tasmania, 1821–December 1825* (Sydney, 1921).
3. 'The Late Mr. Wm. Fletcher', *Hobart Mercury*, September 14, 1872, 2.
4. Ian Morrison, 'Tales of the Unexpected', Tasmanian Archive and Heritage Blog (16 September 2019), https://archivesandheritageblog.libraries.tas.gov.au/tales-of-the-unexpected/.
5. Douglas Stewart Fine Books summary page found within Music: three bound folios of sheet music belonging to Mrs William Fletcher, 1834, Allport Library and Museum of Fine Arts.
6. Ian Morrison, 'Tales of the Unexpected', Tasmanian Archive and Heritage Blog (16 September 2019), https://archivesandheritageblog.libraries.tas.gov.au/tales-of-the-unexpected/.
7. Trove, 'Music: [three bound folios of sheet music belonging to Mrs. William Fletcher, Hobart, 1834]', https://trove.nla.gov.au/work/194114578?keyword=mrs%20w%20fletcher%20folios.
8. *Hobart Town Courier*, July 5, 1833, 3.
9. *Hobart Town Courier*, September 25, 1830, p.2.
10. *Hobart Town Courier*, July 4, 1829, p.1.
11. *Austral-Asiatic Review*, October 15, 1833, p.1.
12. *Colonist and Van Diemen's Land Commercial and Agricultural Advertiser*, July 6, 1832, 1.

13. Michael Sprod, 'Andrew Bent', *The Companion to Tasmanian History*, https://www.utas.edu.au/library/companion_to_tasmanian_history/B/Andrew%20Bent.htm.
14. E Morris Miller, *Pressmen and Governors: Australian Editors and Writers in Early Tasmania* (Sydney, 1973), 81.
15. Michael Sprod, 'Andrew Bent', *The Companion to Tasmanian History*, https://www.utas.edu.au/library/companion_to_tasmanian_history/B/Andrew%20Bent.htm.
16. Clifford Craig, *The Engravers of Van Diemen's Land* (Launceston, 1961), 6.
17. James Ross (1786–1838), Australian Dictionary of Biography, National Centre of Biography, Australian National University, (published first in hardcopy 1967) https://adb.anu.edu.au/biography/ross-james-2607
18. Clifford Craig, *The Engravers of Van Diemen's Land* (Launceston, 1961), 7.
19. Stefan Petrow, 'The life and death of the Hobart Town Mechanics' Institute 1827–1871', *Papers and Proceedings: Tasmanian Historical Research Association*, 40:1 (1993), 9.
20. *Colonial Times*, November 12, 1833, 2.
21. James Ross (1786–1838), Australian Dictionary of Biography, National Centre of Biography, Australian National University, (published first in hardcopy 1967) https://adb.anu.edu.au/biography/ross-james-2607.
22. Leora Auslander, 'The Gendering of Consumer Practices in Nineteenth-Century France', in Victoria de Grazia and Ellen Furlough, eds., *The Sex of Things: Gender and Consumption in Historical Perspective* (Los Angeles, 1996), 103.
23. Leonore Davidoff, Jean L'Esperance and Howard Newby, 'Landscape with Figures: Home and Community in English Society' in Juliet Mitchell and Ann Oakley, eds., *The Rights and Wrongs of Women* (Aylesbury, 1976), 155.
24. Anne McClintock, *Imperial Leather: Race, Gender, and Sexuality in the Colonial Contest* (New York, 1995), 161.
25. Leora Auslander, 'The Gendering of Consumer Practices in Nineteenth-Century France', in Victoria de Grazia and Ellen Furlough, eds., *The Sex of Things: Gender and Consumption in Historical Perspective* (Los Angeles, 1996), 83.
26. Antoinette Burton, 'Toward Unsettling Histories of Domesticity', *American Historical Review*, 124:4 (2019), 1332.
27. Victoria Haskins and Margaret D Jacobs, 'Introduction', *Special Issue: Domestic Frontiers: The Home and Colonization in Frontiers: A Journal of Women Studies*, 28:1&2 (2007), ix.
28. Sara Upstone, 'Domesticity in Magical-Realist Postcolonial Fiction', *Special Issue: Domestic Frontiers: The Home and Colonization in Frontiers: A Journal of Women Studies*, 28:1&2 (2007), 267.
29. Patrizia di Bello, 'Mrs Birkbeck's Album: the Hand-Written and the Printed in Early Nineteenth-Century Feminine Culture', *Interdisciplinary Studies in the Long Nineteenth Century*, 1 (2005), 20.
30. Jeanice Brooks, 'Musical Monuments for the Country House: Music, Collection, and Display at Tatton Park', *Music & Letters*, 91:4 (2010), 523.
31. Ibid, 515.

Theatre Royal Hobart

The architectural influence of William Gore Elliston,
John Lee Archer and Samuel Beazley
and their passion for the Arts

ANNE LEE-ARCHER

The Theatre Royal Hobart is a popular topic. Much has been written about it, from the illustrious actors who trod its boards, through to its lighting and mechanics and its convict theatregoers. However, it is lesser known that the founding members held a deep passion for theatre and personal experience in the arts. This was a force that drove them to build a theatre, not only to have a positive impact on society, but for their personal enjoyment. This article will begin to delve into the lives of two friends who worked together to help create the Theatre Royal, William Gore Elliston and John Lee Archer, and suggest there may have been an influence from another of their friends and colleagues, the renowned theatre architect and playwright in England and Ireland, Samuel Beazley.

■

John Lee Archer (1791–1852) was born in Chatham, Kent, England, on April 26, 1791.[1] He came from a long line of master carpenters, bricklayers, surveyors, architects and engineers, on both his father's and mother's side. He spent his first 27 years living and working in England. He studied for his apprenticeship under surveyor Charles Beazley, worked for Charles' nephew Samuel Beazley and then attained a position as a drawing clerk in the office of renowned engineer and architect, John Rennie. He worked his way up to assistant engineer for Rennie then moved to Dublin, where he worked for seven years (1819–1825). John Lee Archer was appointed by Lord Bathurst and the Crown to the position of Civil Engineer of Van Diemen's Land in December 1826. He sailed for Van Diemen's Land on the *Lang*, arriving in Hobart on August 2, 1827.[2] He was Australia's first civil engineer. On August 8, Governor Arthur announced that he was adding Architect for the Colony to Archer's engineering role.[3] Archer was responsible for the architectural design and structural engineering of all government buildings. His duties included the construction and repair of public buildings, churches, convict and military barracks, hospitals, lighthouses, bridges, wharves, causeways and more. He held this position until 1839 when the engineering department was unfairly restructured, but that's a whole other story!

Back to the Theatre Royal. What is more fascinating is John Lee Archer's untold passion for Shakespeare and his work with theatre architect and playwright, Samuel Beazley.

According to John Lee Archer's personal diary, during his teenage years and early 20s, he lived for some time in the house of Charles Beazley, to whom he was apprenticed, at Chelsea.[4] Samuel Beazley, the theatre architect, was the nephew of Charles Beazley. Samuel designed two Lyceum theatres (1816 and 1834), new Theatre Royal in Birmingham (1820), Dublin Theatre Royal (1821), and remodelled Drury Lane (1822), St James's (1835), City of London Theatre (1837) and many more.[5]

Samuel had two sisters, Nancy and Emily. They were living at Chelsea at the same time as John Lee Archer. There are numerous entries in Archer's diary relating to the Beazleys, theatres and fairs which were also places people went to see theatre performed. See a small selection in the table following. John Lee Archer visits Shakespeare's grave at Stratford Upon Avon and even mentions acting in two Shakespeare plays in London, Banquo in *Macbeth* and Lodovico in *Othello*.

> 26 April 1811
> A Farce called the Boarding house produced at the Lyceum written by Sam:
>
> 2 Sep 1811
> Alarm at the Lyceum this Evening (Theatre Falling) Sam: spoke from stage.
>
> 2 Jan 1812
> Went to Epsom to assist Sams Clerks Surveying a few days.

31 Aug 1812
: With Sam. Beazley from Town to Edgeware—Surveying there.

19 April 1813
: Walk to Town from Epsom Morning (last time for Sam:)—

2 Nov 1814
: Waited on C. Beazley and signed Sams Letter of License—

28 August 1815
: Sutton St. Private Theatre. Evening. Rogers's debut.

9 Oct 1815
: Berwick St. Private Theatre—Rogers—as Stukely—Usher, Emma and Mrs Love there—

1 April 1817
: Minors evening. Memo: <u>Banquo</u> My first appearance.

12 August 1817
: With Rogers. Italian Opera—<u>Don Giovanni</u>

29 September 1817
: Walk. Richmond—Theatre. Mrs Robinson's Juliet—Walk Town after.

29 January 1818
: Wilson Street Evening Othello—first appearance (<u>Lodovico</u>)

26 October 1818
: At Stratford upon Avon—Visited Shakespeare's grave. Arrived at Birmingham.

"Rog" was his friend William Rogers, who was also a surveyor and architect who studied under Charles Beazley and worked for John Rennie. John Lee Archer called his fourth son, William Rogers Lee Archer in his name. The three architects, John Lee Archer, William Rogers and Samuel Beazley, with their practical knowledge of the stage, must have discussed how to improve theatre and acoustic design. The Theatre Royal Hobart apparently has very good acoustics. That is not a coincidence.

In 1818, John Lee Archer moved to Dublin. Coincidentally (or is it?) Samuel Beazley was commissioned to design the Theatre Royal Dublin, with the first stone laid on October 14, 1820, and the grand opening 65 days later on January 18, 1821. Up to 700 workers were employed.[6] It is not known if

The New Theatre Royal, Dublin, 1821. Architect, Samuel Beazley.
Artist, George Petrie. Reproduced courtesy of the National Library of Ireland.

John Lee Archer had any involvement in the Theatre Royal Dublin, but it is entirely possible that he conducted some surveys prior to the foundation stone being laid, or site visits during construction for Sam in his absence. If nothing else, he would have had a personal interest in following the project and definitely would have attended the theatre, gleaning ideas that he brought out to Van Diemen's Land.

When John Lee Archer arrived in Van Diemen's Land, his passion for theatre and in particular Shakespeare, continued. He called his home Jutland House, a reference to both his hometown in Kent that was settled by the Jutes in ancient times and also Macbeth, who ruled Jutland. According to his diary, we know that in 1837 John Lee Archer named his horse Jemmy. Given his love of Shakespeare, Jemmy was probably a black horse, referring to a scene in Shakespeare's *Edward III* where Douglas says, "Jemmy, my man, saddle my bonny black."[7]

He became friends with William Gore Elliston, possibly through the Masonic Lodge. John Lee Archer was initiated on June 24, 1832, obtained his Master Mason degree on November 7, 1832, became Senior Warden in 1834 and Worshipful Master in 1836. Records are scant, but we know that William Gore Elliston was secretary in 1833 and may have held other positions.

Apparently the first professional dramatic performance in Hobart was held at the Freemasons' Tavern in December 1833:

> Saloon theatres ... were not licensed to perform 'legitimate drama' ... and it is not surprising that a proposal was made to erect a more appropriate building for the presentation of 'legitimate drama' in Hobart. One, also, that could accommodate more than the 150 patrons which was all the Freemasons' could seat.[8]

Degraves also detailed that the Freemasons' Lodge at the bottom of Harrington Street was too narrow to change scenery easily and female actors could not change their clothes decently.[9] Subscribers were canvassed, money raised and Governor Arthur's support obtained to ensure the theatre would be officially approved with a royal patent, allowing it to present serious drama.[10]

William Gore Elliston (1798–1892) emigrated to Van Diemen's Land in January 1830. He tried his hand at school teaching and auctioneering, and also owned a store and spirit warehouse. He is probably best known for owning and editing the *Hobart Town Courier, Hobart Town Almanack* and *Van Diemen's Land Annual*. Later in life he entered politics, becoming a Justice of the Peace, Commissioner of the City of Hobart, member of the Legislative Council and second mayor of Hobart (1855), and was usher of the Black Rod in 1869.[11] What is more pertinent to the Theatre Royal Hobart's history, is his upbringing in theatrical life in England and his ongoing passion for music and the arts. In his obituary it stated he " ... was well versed in Shakespeare and other plays, which made his father so famous".[12] He gave dramatic readings and was also an amateur vocalist. He performed in John Philip Deane's concert in Hobart in January 1832, singing Waller's *The Soldier's Tear* and Bishop's *Sons of Freedom*.[13]

> On Monday the lovers of music enjoyed the greatest treat that ever was given in this Colony—it was Mr. J. P. Deane's sixth concert. The capacious Court-house was crowded to excess—no less than 250 persons were present; among others we noticed His Excellency the Lieutenant Governor, Mrs. Arthur, and family ... Mr. Elliston gave "The Soldier's Tear" of Bayley's in a most exquisite manner. We have seldom heard a song where more expression was given by the performer—it was rapturously encored ... Mr. Elliston was

encored in his second song of "Sons of Freedom"—but of the two performances we are decidedly of opinion that his first was the most exquisite …[14]

William Gore Elliston was born on October 17, 1798, in Bath, the eldest son of actor and theatre manager, Robert William Elliston (1774–1831) and dancing teacher, Elizabeth Rundall. Robert William Elliston was theatre royalty at the time. To understand the standing of William's father, one has to remember that in the early 1800s, plays were a form of entertainment and actors were similar to film stars. In a search for "Robert William Elliston" at the National Portrait Gallery in England, there are 24 sketches of him performing

William Gore Elliston's father, Robert William Elliston, as Frank Heartall in Cherry's *The Soldier's Daughter*, 1818.
© *The National Portrait Gallery, London*

in varied roles, providing an insight into the depth and breadth of his skill.[15] He left home and started acting in Bath, followed by Leeds and Bristol and then back to Bath where he obtained regular work between London and Bath, with all the leading business being gradually assigned to him.

Lord Byron believed he was inimitable in high comedy; and Macready praised his versatility.[16] So great was the popularity of Elliston as an actor, that an audience once broke through the doors of His Majesty's Theatre in Haymarket, West End, London, storming the theatre to see him perform.[17] Dramatic critic, Leigh Hunt in his book on the actors of the time, declared Elliston "the only genius that has approached that great actor (Garrick) in universality of imitation", and said he was better at comedy than tragedy, but was "the second tragedian on the stage" (to Kemble) and spoke in awe of his ability to overcome his lack of tragedian looks. He acknowledged that "Mr Elliston's peculiar warmth of feeling has rendered him the best lover on the stage both in tragedy and comedy".[18]

Elliston also managed theatres, including those in Wells, Shepton Mallet, Manchester, Birmingham and in London—Little Drury Lane (later called Olympic Pavilion), Leicester Theatre, Surrey Theatre and Drury Lane.

Elliston was friends with Samuel Beazley:

> One of Elliston's principal advisers at this time was Mr. Beazley, a gentleman whose active and intelligent qualities in his profession, as architect and dramatic writer, have gained him considerable renown. Mr. Beazley's social temperament was also well appreciated by one who was himself the best company; so that hours of business were by no means the only time they discussed together; and few things, either by day or night, came amiss to the available temper of our modern Vanburgh.[19]

Beazley was commissioned by Elliston to design grand assembly rooms and a library at Leamington Spa. His son William Gore Elliston owned and managed the Reading Room, until it was sold. Beazley also remodelled Drury Lane for Elliston in 1822.

Sadly, Robert William Elliston was declared bankrupt in 1826, suffered ill health and epileptic seizures, and died July 7, 1831. Samuel Beazley was present at the funeral and was such a close friend he was listed as family.[20]

His son William Gore Elliston decided to emigrate and arrived in Hobart aboard the *Chatham* in January 1830. He married Margaret (b. 1807), youngest daughter of Daniel de Vaux of London, on February 25, 1832.[21] In his personal diary he mentions spending quite some time with John Lee Archer.

> 28 September 1832
> Breakfasted with J.L Archer at Giants Castle after which rode a mile or two into the bush to Sassafras Valley. Returned and paid a visit to the orphan school—took a chop at the "Castle" and rode to town making a call at the allotment.[22]

The orphan school refers to the St John's Church and orphanage at New Town. Construction took place between 1831–1833 and was one of John Lee Archer's most notable works. Elliston mentions in his diary travelling with Archer to the Iron Pot lighthouse in November 1834, another Archer design. See other diary entries below:

> Thursday 1 January 1835
> Dined with C Reid my old ship mate—rode out to New Town called on John Lee Archer where I slept the night.
> Friday 2 January 1835
> Went into town bought a pair of spurs returned and dined at John Lee Archers and slept there
> Saturday 3 January 1835
> Was to leave town today but Archer could not get his official business completed on Friday—rode into town—called on Dan Sutton who gave me his two acceptances at 3 and 6 months for £35 each
> Sunday 4 January 1835
> Still at Archers
> Monday 5 January 1835
> Started at 5 o'clock in the morning accompanied by J.L Archer. Reached New Newfolk 1/4 p 8 to breakfast. Visited the Hospital, Jail and Police Office and Church—proceeded on to Hamilton examined the foundation of the new church there—drank tea with the Police Magistrate Torlese Esq.[23]

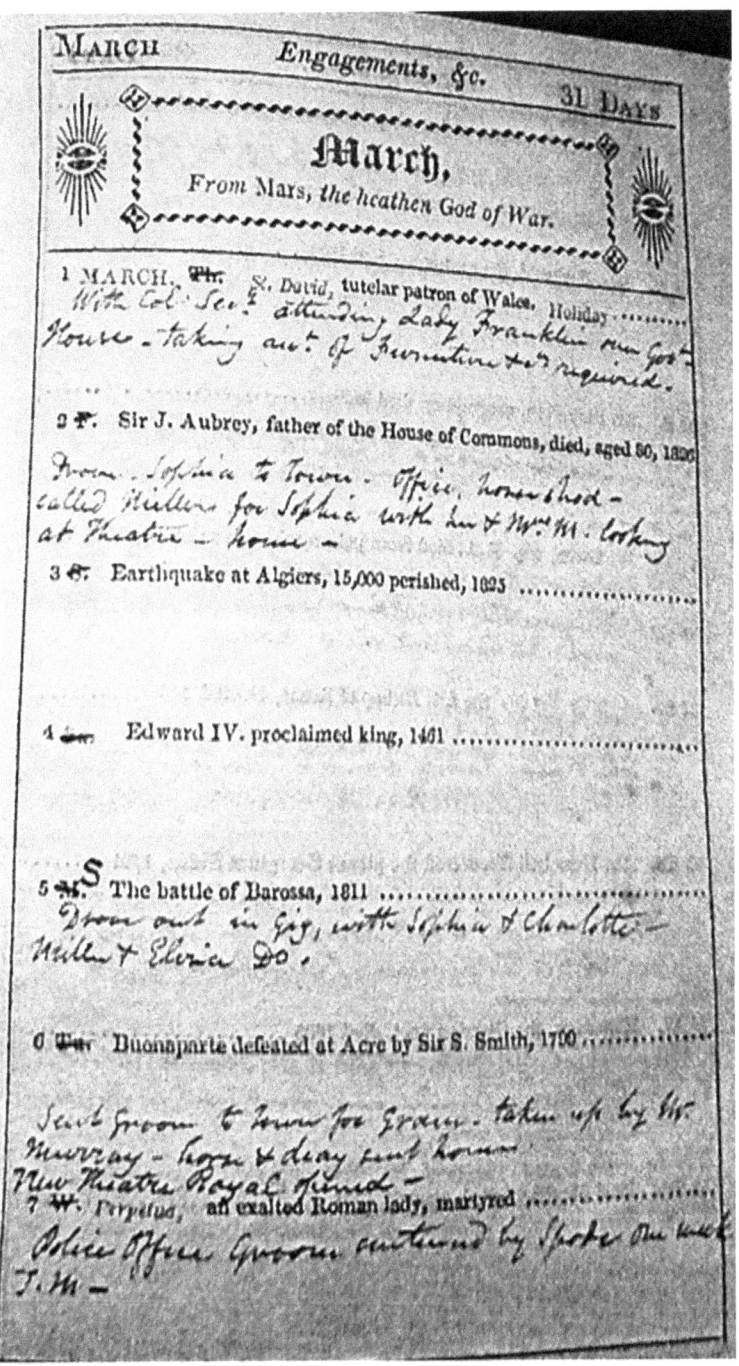

John Lee Archer's personal diary, 1836–37, referencing the Theatre Royal and William Gore Elliston.

Archives of Tasmania

> 8 Th. Sir W. Chambers, architect, of Somerset-house, died 1796........
> with Sophia, Miller, Eliza & Mrs Miller to the Theatre
> Col. Elliston & wife in same Box —

Archer's entry in his diary for March 8, 1837
Archives of Tasmania

Similarly, Archer mentions Elliston in his personal diary. Two days after the theatre was opened, they took their families to the theatre and sat in one of the boxes together.

31 December 1836

Newtown Church early morning—office etc. as usual—N.S.—Theatre—Eliza 12 months this day—same height as Charlotte at a year old.

2 January 1837

Called on Elliston Courier Office—Saw Mrs Elliston—N.O. Store—Office afternoon—Sent drawings of Court House Launceston to Col. Secretary—Theatre—Home.

4 January 1837

Office N.S—Cold day—Called Courier Office—Mr & Mrs E and Dr Ross there.

6 January 1837

Sir John Franklin arrived in the Fairlie—Government House morning with Sophia saw the landing of The Governor—Elliston's after, lunch-home.

8 January 1837

Hot wind all day—Elliston and family came out and dined—slight rain evening—didn't go out.

20 January 1837

Capt., Rebecca & William left for Gordons—office—home, in gig with Sophia and Charlotte to Town—called Ellistons—Spode spoke to me about Messenger—S.N.

2 March 1837

> Drove Sophia to Town—office, horse shod—called Millers for Sophia. With Mr & Mrs M[24] looking at Theatre-house

6 March 1837
> Sent Groom to Town for Grain—taken up by Mr Murray—horse and dray sent home. New Theatre Royal opened

8 March 1837
> With Sophia, Miller, Eliza and Mrs Miller to the Theatre Evening. Elliston and wife in same box.

1 April 1837
> Elliston on Jemmy—rode with him to Brown's river dined with Lucas family—returned by the new road—much tired—Elliston's—home.

There are various other entries throughout the year, detailing dinners, spending the day together, visiting both Mr & Mrs Elliston with his wife Sophia and daughter Eliza in their gig, but he definitely visited Elliston more often in the month before the theatre opened. They probably had much to discuss!

A person by the name of "The Odd Man Out" in the *Critic* newspaper in 1916 described John Lee Archer as, "the architect of the Theatre Royal, Campbell Street".[25] The Theatre Royal was not known as an Archer design and he had completed many significant buildings. To single that one out and use it as his defining building appears to be deliberate and pointed. Peter Degraves himself wrote a letter in 1846 to the Colonial Secretary suggesting that there was more involvement by Archer as the architect than originally thought. "A Theatrical Committee was appointed and I was requested to furnish a plan, elevation and section: which having been approved of by Mr. John Lee Archer (the Honorary Architect) my plan, and tender was accepted …"[26] Wilfred Hudspeth stated that Degraves "was not however a professional architect. At one of the meetings held by the promoters, a plan of the proposed theatre, at an estimated cost of £2000, was produced by a Mr Archer. This may have been the plan adopted by De Graves."[27] Whether or not John Lee Archer produced the design, approved it, or both, we will never know for sure. However, he was definitely involved in the design in some way.

So why the smoke and mirrors? To understand, we need to look beyond the theatre at the accusations, controversy and fearmongering of the time. Governor Arthur forbade any government employee from doing any work for

> a Theatrical Committee was appointed, and I was requested to furnish a plan, elevation, and section: which having been approved of by Mr. John Lee Archer (the honorary Architect) my plan, and tender was accepted, and the structure being half built only – a disasterous change in the times took place, the subscriptions were not half paid up – I was £2500 in advance with a mortgage

Peter Degraves' letter to Colonial Secretary, February 11, 1846.
Tasmanian Archives, Correspondence, "A" Series, CSO20-1-12, file 270

individuals or private enterprise. There was a Government Order on July 10, 1832, for a full investigation into the engineering department and the King's Yard to investigate the use of government bricks, lumber and employees.[28] There was also a court case where Roderick O'Connor and John Lee Archer were called to testify as witnesses.[29] It was in this turbulent political environment that discussions about the theatre began. No doubt, John Lee Archer wanted to be involved, but requested to be kept out of the limelight and deliberately made sure his name was not mentioned in any documents.

It will be impossible to prove, but it would make for an interesting study for experts in theatre architecture to compare Beazley's theatres with the Theatre Royal Hobart's original design from the descriptions available. Wilfred Hudspeth believed it was similar to the Theatre Royal Bath.[30] If that is the case, then perhaps it was not Samuel Beazley who influenced the design. William Gore Elliston was born in Bath and his father had a regular acting job there, so Elliston may have tried to recreate the theatre he loved from his childhood and John Lee Archer designed it with his knowledge gleaned from working with Beazley. The Theatre Royal Hobart's history is a comedy and a tragedy all rolled into one intriguing mystery.

. . .

NOTES

1. *Chatham St. Mary Parish Records—Christenings*, Reference 85. Date 1568–1974. Medway Ancestors Imagebase—Image 00020114. 1791. N.p.: Medway Archives.
2. *Colonial Times and Tasmanian Advertiser (Hobart Tas: 1825–1827)*. 1827. "Ship News." August 3, 1827, 2.
3. *The Hobart Town Gazette (Tas.: 1825–1833)*. 1827. "Government Notice." August 11, 1827, 2. https://nla.gov.au/nla.news-article8791634.
4. John L Archer. 1808–1818. *Personal Diary*, London Years. Held by descendants on the Murray line of the family. Accessed in person and photographed.
5. Görel Garlick. 2003. *To serve the purpose of the drama: the theatre designs and plays of Samuel Beazley, 1786–1851*. N.p.: Society for Theatre Research.
6. Görel Garlick. 2003. *To serve the purpose of the drama: the theatre designs and plays of Samuel Beazley, 1786–1851*. N.p.: Society for Theatre Research.
7. William Shakespeare. n.d. *Edward III*, Act 1, Scene 2. Accessed September 19, 2022. http://shakespearestudyguide.com/EdwardIIItext.html.
8. Gillian Winter. 1985. "A colonial theatrical experience: the Royal Victoria Theatre, Hobart, 1837/ 1857." *Papers and Proceedings: Tasmanian Historical Research Association* 32, no. 4 (December), 121–145.
9. Ross Thorne. 1977. "Hobart's historic Royal." *Theatre Australia* 2, no. 2 (June), 16–19.
10. *The Mercury*. 1902. "Old Time Theatricals—Story Of The Theatre Royal." November 6, 1902, 6.
11. JW Beattie. n.d. "Biography—William Gore Elliston—Australian Dictionary of Biography." Australian Dictionary of Biography. Accessed September 17, 2022. https://adb.anu.edu.au/biography/elliston-william-gore-2024.
12. *The Mercury*. 1872. "William Gore Elliston". December 5, 1872.
13. William Walker. n.d. "Australharmony—Biographical register E." The University of Sydney. Accessed September 19, 2022. https://www.sydney.edu.au/paradisec/australharmony/register-E.php.
14. *Colonial Times (Hobart, Tas.: 1828–1857)*. 1832. "Hobart Town." January 11, 1832. https://nla.gov.au/nla.news-article8646254.
15. National Portrait Gallery London. n.d. "Robert William Elliston". National Portrait Gallery. Accessed September 17, 2022. https://npgimages.com/search/?searchQuery=robert+william+elliston.
16. "Robert William Elliston". n.d. Wikipedia. Accessed September 18, 2022. https://en.wikipedia.org/wiki/Robert_William_Elliston.
17. George Raymond. 1857. *The Life and Enterprises of Robert William Elliston*. London: G. Routledge Company.
18. Leigh Hunt. 1894. *Dramatic Essays*. London: Walter Scott Ltd.
19. Sir John Vanbrugh was an English architect, dramatist and herald, perhaps best known as the designer of Blenheim Palace and Castle Howard; Raymond, George. 1857. *The Life and Enterprises of Robert William Elliston*. London: G Routledge Company.
20. George Raymond. 1857. *The Life and Enterprises of Robert William Elliston*. London: G Routledge Company.

21. JW Beattie. n.d. "Biography—William Gore Elliston". Australian Dictionary of Biography. Accessed September 17, 2022. https://adb.anu.edu.au/biography/elliston-william-gore-2024.
22. William G Elliston. 1832–1835. *William Gore Elliston's Personal Diary*, Diary in the possession of descendent, Robert William Elliston II at Ross Creek Victoria, Australia. Visited in person August 2006.
23. William G Elliston. 1832–1835. *William Gore Elliston's Personal Diary*, Diary in the possession of descendent, Robert William Elliston II at Ross Creek Victoria, Australia. Visited in person August 2006.
24. Mr & Mrs M refers to Mr & Mrs Miller. John Lee Archer's wife was Sophia Mattinson. Sophia's sister, Eliza Mattinson married Henry Miller. Mr & Mrs Miller either refers to Henry and Eliza or to Henry's parents, Henry and Jane Miller.
25. *Critic (Hobart, Tas.: 1907–1924)*. 1916. "Notes by the Way (By 'The Odd Man Out')." April 8, 1916, 3.
26. Ross Thorne. 1977. "Hobart's historic Royal." *Theatre Australia* 2, no. 2 (June): 16–19.
27. Roy Smith. n.d. *Roy Smith Papers*. N.p.: Held at Launceston Library Special Collections.
28. John Burnett. 1832. *Government Order*, CSO 1/603/13753. N.p.: Tasmanian Archives.
29. *R v Gregson*, court case, 1832.
30. Michael Roe. 1960. *A History Of The Theatre Royal Hobart From 1834*. Hobart: Law Society of Tasmania.

"Pardoned to serve His Majesty by sea"

The life of George Briggs

GUY SALVIDGE

I first encountered the name of sealer George Briggs in James Boyce's peerless history *Van Diemen's Land*. Employed by Captain James Kelly on a whaleboat circumnavigating Tasmania in 1815–16, Briggs is said to have been the key negotiator between Kelly's crew and the Aboriginal Tasmanians they met during the journey.[1] KM Bowden provides a fuller account based on the writings of Kelly himself: "At noon [we] landed at Ringarooma Point. Here we suddenly fell in with a large "mob" of natives, who, upon their first appearance seemed hostile, but on seeing Briggs, who they knew particularly well [...] seemed delighted."[2] Briggs is said to have "left two wives and five children upon the islands", one of the wives being "a daughter of the chief Lamanbunganah."[3] When Lamanbunganah asked for assistance in fighting another chief, his brother Tolobunganah, Briggs declined. "At this Laman seemed greatly dissatisfied, and told Briggs, in a very hostile tone, that he had often before gone with him to fight other tribes when he (Briggs) wanted women."[4] Briggs, we are told, managed to dodge this responsibility without being drawn into conflict and the whaleboat voyage continued unimpeded.

In their histories, Boyce and Bowden have drawn upon a narrative by James Kelly published in 1854 as "Some unrecorded passages in the history of Van Diemen's Land. (From a very old stager.)" Kelly's account offers a fascinating insight into an important chapter in Tasmanian history, but it is also problematic. Kelly was hardly a disinterested observer and likely shaped his work to present himself and his crew in a favourable light. Famed for his exaggerations and tall tales later in life, Kelly "once won a bet that his trousers would hold five bushels of wheat".[5] Kelly's claim to have measured the length of a man's leap at 11 yards is absurd,[6] and his description of George Town seems dubious. He describes visiting the government cottage, barracks and storehouse at George Town in January 1816,[7] in contrast to Governor Macquarie's lament of more than a year later that the works had "made very slow progress".[8] In June 1817, Lieutenant-Governor Sorell reported to Macquarie that there is "no Building erected [at George Town] but a temporary Store and a Lime Hut",[9] casting doubt on the veracity of Kelly's narrative.

Despite these reservations, I was nevertheless intrigued about George Briggs and wanted to know more. Websites such as *Trove* and *FamilySearch* aggregate a wealth of material unavailable to previous generations of researchers, and thus we discover that George William Christopher Lamuel Briggs was born in the town of Dunstable in England in June 1787.[10] His parents were William Briggs and Mary Jane Simms and he was baptised on December 31, 1788, the eldest of nine children.[11] On July 12, 1800, shortly after his thirteenth birthday, Briggs was convicted in London at Newgate Prison on a charge of piracy. Instead of facing execution, George (listed here as Geo Briggs) was instead "Pardoned to serve His Majesty by sea".[12]

Extract from Briggs' prison record

We can only surmise how this might have happened. It is not specified where Briggs was arrested, but it was probably in London and not Dunstable, his piratical deeds on the muddy banks of the Thames. David Wells explains that, at this time, "[c]rime on the river was rife [as] one third of the people employed in dock labour were engaged in some form of criminal activity".[13] The lowest rung on the criminal ladder was the mudlark, usually a small boy whose task it was to linger in the mud at low tide and retrieve goods thrown down from nearby ships. These thefts cost merchants an estimated £500,000 per year (£53,000,000 in today's money).[14] In 1798, London magistrates established the

Marine Police to curb such piracy, and the scheme proved so successful that founder Patrick Colquhoun was able to boast a saving of £122,000 in the first year.[15] Young George Briggs may well have run afoul of the world's first police force.

Historians Brian Plomley and Kristen Anne Henley contend that Briggs was born in England and "arrived at Port Jackson on the *Harrington* on March 4, 1805".[16] This is in contradiction to Bowden, who describes Briggs as "native born", that is born in the New South Wales colony.[17] *Harrington* was a 150 or 180-ton brig with a complicated history, captured by the French and returned to the British in time to sail from Madras in 1801 under the command of William Campbell.[18] When *Harrington* arrived in Sydney that June, Governor King refused to allow its cargo of 4,000 gallons of spirits to be landed.[19] Over the next year, *Harrington* was engaged in sealing activity in Bass Strait, Norfolk Island and King Island, landing a party of 12 Englishmen on New Year Island off King Island.[20] By the time the French corvettes *Le Géographe* and *Le Naturaliste* arrived at King Island in December 1802, the *Harrington* sealers had been there 13 months. Is it possible that George Briggs was among them, and that Plomley and Henley were mistaken in believing him to have arrived in Australia in 1805?

Sent in a longboat to circumnavigate King Island, French surveyor Pierre Faure spent three days in the company of the *Harrington* sealers.[21] If Briggs was among them, then he was present at a remarkable event and one that played a critical part in the subsequent colonisation of Tasmania. Governor King sent Lieutenant Charles Robbins to intercept the French at King Island, where Robbins infamously (and presumably accidentally) flew the Union Jack upside down over the French tents as a means of pressing the British claim over Van Diemen's Land.[22] Within two years, the British had established colonies on the Derwent in the south and the Tamar in the north of the island.

There was also money to be made. It is a little-known fact that Australia's first export commodity was sealskins. After the wreck of the *Sydney Cove* on Preservation Island in 1797, salvage efforts were made not only to rescue the sailors languishing there, but to retrieve the ship's valuable cargo of rum. Explorer Matthew Flinders was aboard one such voyage and discovered "the great seal rookeries of the Furneaux, and other groups lying in the eastern end of Bass Strait".[23] The following year, Captain Bishop of the *Nautilus* led a sealing venture to nearby Cape Barren Island, yielding "9000 seal skins of the first quality and several tons of oil", a cargo which eventually sold for $14,000 in Canton.²⁴ Such skins were durable and waterproof, making excellent caps, capes and stoles, and were highly sought after on the Chinese and London markets where they sold for upward of a pound apiece. *Harrington* brought 3,000 sealskins to Sydney in December 1801 and a further 5,200 the following June. By December 1804, Sydney firm Kable & Underwood had brought in 32,000 skins and, along with William Campbell, were said to employ 180 sealers in Bass Strait.²⁵ By October 1805, 216 men were working as sealers, a figure which constituted 10–15 per cent of the free men in the colony.²⁶

But while profits for the sealing masters were considerable, working conditions for sealers were often hellish.

> It is difficult to appreciate the demands, physical and emotional, of the roller-coaster ride that was primitive Georgian sealing. Approaching coasts we wouldn't venture near today in much more buoyant craft, these men, many of whom couldn't swim, pulled oars on heavy, timber boats, stormed ashore on the crest of a wave, stood backs to an often-treacherous sea, clubbing and stabbing in bawling frenzy, while angry, frightened, biting animals tried to stampede past, throwing hundreds of pounds of blubber and teeth behind a headlong rush to the ocean. Even success meant long hours of stench and butchery, risky clambering with heavy pelts over unforgiving, slippery stone, loading tossing, perilous, egg-shell casks into pitching, foundering clinker boats.²⁷

Worse, sealers were often paid by a "lay" system whereby they would receive a percentage of the skins taken over the course of a voyage in lieu of wages. A 1/100th lay was common. Deducted from this were expenses incurred for items such as food, clothing and tobacco, and thus it was not uncommon for sealers to become heavily indebted to their masters despite their months-long labour.²⁸

Once the seals had been slain, "a hooked device would drag the carcass before the skin was removed, usually in one piece (feet, snout and eyeholes intact), and then pegged out to dry and treated with salt".²⁹ Seal oil was a valuable commodity, procured by melting blubber in a cast iron trypot and then draining the oil into casks. Elephant seals were especially prized for their oil, three gallons of which might fetch a pound at market. As an adult bull yielded as much as 17 gallons, this was a lucrative albeit short-lived business.³⁰

The short-sightedness of the English sealers was apparent to the French as early as 1802, Commandant Baudin observing that "[t]here is every sign that in a short while your fishermen will have drained [King Island] of its resources through the hunting of the fur seals and the sea elephants [...] in a little while you will hear it said that they have entirely disappeared."[31] By 1810, the elephant seals of King Island had been hunted near to extinction and the rookeries of the Furneaux lay devastated.

Whether George Briggs was a party to this wholesale slaughter is not known, but fragments of his later career can be assembled by way of the shipping notices in the *Sydney Gazette and New South Wales Advertiser*, especially if we accept that George Briggs, George Buggs and George Baggs were the same man.[32] Thus we discover a George Buggs departing Sydney aboard the schooner *Governor Hunter* on April 14, 1805.[33] On December 8, of that year, *Governor Hunter* is again "ready to proceed to Bass's Straits" with George Baggs among its crew.[34] In the New South Wales General Muster of 1806, Briggs is listed as "Sealing" in "Kable employ" in the category "EC" (Emancipated Convict).[35] "Kable employ" refers to Henry Kable, a renowned Sydney businessman and ex-convict who had partnered with boatbuilder James Underwood in forming a successful trading enterprise.

Extract from 1806 NSW General Muster

Briggs might have continued sealing for the Sydney traders for many years, except for an event that was to alter the course of his life. Listed under his correct name, Briggs is named as departing Sydney aboard *Governor Hunter* on November 6, 1808.[36] On July 30, 1809, the *Gazette* reported that the *Governor Hunter* had run aground on Badger Island, off north-east Tasmania, on April 1.[37] Owner Isaac Nichols purchased another ship to sail to the rescue and *Governor Hunter* was refloated and returned to Sydney in April 1810 after an absence of nearly 18 months.[38] This gives rise to a simple question: did Briggs take this opportunity to flee his sealing masters and make a life for himself in Van Diemen's Land?

It is at this point that Briggs is said to have been the first sealer to make his home on lungtalanana (Clarke Island), less than 20 kilometres from where

> **SHIP NEWS.**
>
> On Tuesday arrived the very fine colonial schooner Governor Hunter, Mr. Nichols owner, with about 2000 prime seal skins, after an absence of 17 months. This vessel was equipped for the seal trade; and on her pursuits was in a gale of wind driven on shore into Badger Island, Bass's Straits, on the 1st of April, 1808; the intelli-

Excerpt from the *Sydney Gazette and New South Wales Advertiser*

Governor Hunter ran aground.[39] Briggs is thought to have been in contact with the pairrebeenne clan of the tebrakunna (Cape Portland) region of north-east Tasmania.[40] The chief of this clan, Mannalargenna, is said to have given his daughter Woretemoeteyenner to Briggs in marriage, suggesting that Mannalargenna is the chieftain named Lamanbunganah in Kelly's narrative. The nature of this marriage is disputed, however. As Plomley and Henley would have it, Briggs abducted his bride (whom they name Waremodeenner), sired several children by her, and then sold her to another sealer, John Thomas, for a guinea sometime after 1820.[41] Surely this is the "African slave trade in miniature" that George Robinson railed against two decades later.[42] Perhaps not, as Walter and Daniels explain: "Given that George Briggs learned Woretemoeteyenner's language and was on good terms with her father for many years, it was likely an arrangement rather than a direct abduction."[43] Woretemoeteyenner's life proved even more remarkable, and some of the couple's children led incredible lives in their own right.[44] "Dolly" Dalrymple was born in 1812, Eliza in 1817, Mary in 1818, and John in 1820. Another was fated to die in childhood, however:

> One of these women, who had been for many years attached to a sailor, a young man of respectable connections, but of a wild and volatile disposition, one evening wandered from her sealing party with a young child at her breast, and accidentally falling in with a band of natives, was immediately attacked, and threatened to be severely punished; her infant was snatched from her, and

thrown into a large fire [... the woman] plucked her child from the devouring element and ran off with it into the woods [...] making her escape [and] before morning reached the town of Launceston, a distance of about 10 miles, where she once more found a comfortable home at the residence of a gentleman of that place. This gentleman and his lady, greatly to their credit, had previously taken under their protection, the eldest child of this woman, now a fine girl about 11 years old, and the first child born by a native woman to a white man in Van Diemen's Land. She is called Miss Dalrymple.[45]

Historian Lynette Russell explores the nature of the relationship between English sealers and Tasmanian Aboriginal women in *Roving Mariners*, arguing that she is "seeking an alternative view of this past that disrupts the idea that it can be easily and unproblematically divided into simple dichotomies and binaries of colonizer and colonized".[46] While George Robinson saw only slavery for Tasmanian Aboriginal women, Russell asserts that these women "lived complex lives that shifted and altered over time, sometimes even morphing from captive to partner and wife, all the while maintaining their cultural sense of themselves".[47]

We do not know to what extent Briggs and Woretemoeteyenner considered themselves husband and wife, but uncomfortable facts remain. "Dolly" was baptised Dalrymple Mountgarrett Briggs in Launceston by Reverend Knopwood in 1814,[48] at which time Dolly was not living with her parents but with surgeon Jacob Mountgarrett and his wife Bridget. Briggs' second wife, whom Plomley and Henley call "Meetoneyernanner" or "Dumpe", later lived with another sealer, Tom Tucker.[49] Robinson wrote in his journal that "Dumpe [was] living with Tucker and by whom she has a child living, has killed two children, a boy and a girl, directly after they were born, and [Tucker] beat her plenty with a stick or club".[50] Meanwhile, Woretemoeteyenner was sold to John Thomas for the price of one guinea. While it is difficult to imagine this as anything other than slavery, it is worth noting that it was not only women of Aboriginal descent who were bought and sold in Van Diemen's Land. Alison Alexander points to an incident in 1816 in which a man "brought his wife to hammer" after which "she was sold and delivered to a settler for one gallon of rum and 20 ewes."[51] In Van Diemen's Land, women were often seen as commodities and were frequently treated in a manner we would consider barbaric.

Briggs fades into obscurity after 1816. On June 19, 1819, the pages of the *Hobart Town Gazette* report that "Mr Charles Read proceeding on the Schooner *Sindbad* from Port Dalrymple, requests all claims against him may be presented for payment.—Also George Briggs, servant."[52] In October of that same year, we see Briggs departing Sydney aboard Glory,[53] and in June 1823 he is aboard Nereus, its muster offering our only physical description of the man. Briggs is described as having "hazel eyes, light red hair, fair ruddy complexion and freckles; from Dunstable (Bedfordshire)", later finding work as a "seaman on Griffiths' schooner (June 1831)."[54] *Geneanet* lists Briggs' death as July 11, 1837, and his burial place as Kingston,[55] the latter of which seems unlikely as Kingston, then known as Browns River, was nothing more than a hamlet in 1837. *FamilySearch* would have it that Briggs was buried at Cornelian Bay in Hobart,[56] but this is also unlikely as it did not open until 1872, although some remains from older cemeteries were relocated there. It seems more likely that Briggs' final resting place was in Launceston, although no record has ever been found.

I am a Briggs too, albeit one descended from a different George Briggs. My great-grandmother Mary Ann Briggs was born in Grimsby, Lincolnshire in 1884. Her parents were Thomas and Mary Codd Briggs, born in Lincolnshire in 1843 and 1844. Thomas' parents were George and Catherine Rose Briggs, born in Lincolnshire in 1800 and 1803. My most distant recorded Briggs ancestor is John Briggs, born in 1754. Fourteen years later, George William Christopher Lamuel Briggs' father William was born in Austerfield, South Yorkshire, no more than forty miles from the birthplace of my ancestors. This is not surprising as roughly halfway between Austerfield and Grimsby lies the village of Brigg, ancestral home of the Briggs clan.

Julie Gough, Tasmanian artist and descendent of Woretemoeteyenner and George Briggs, explores the lives of her ancestors in her artwork. Gough's 2007 piece representing the trauma of Woretemoeteyenner's sale consists of a "book sealed shut with a funereal black beaded cover".[57] Gough writes that "[t]his artwork is about the frustration, anxiety and anger that I carry about those times. I am like this closed book; this story is in me, but it is hard to fathom."[58] As difficult and as traumatic as opening this book might be, it is the story of our shared history and one we must call our own.

■ ■ ■

NOTES

1. James Boyce, *Van Diemen's Land* (Melbourne: Black Inc, 2008), 96.
2. KM Bowden, *Captain James Kelly of Hobart Town* (Adelaide: The Griffiths Press, 1964), 36.
3. Ibid.
4. Ibid.
5. ER Pretyman, "Some Notes on the Life and Times of Captain James Kelly," *Papers & Proceedings of the Royal Society of Tasmania,* 1970, Vol. 105, 111.
6. Bowden, *Captain James Kelly*, 31.
7. Ibid., 35.
8. *Historical Records of Australia, Series 3 Vol. 2.* (Sydney: Government Printer, 1921), 192.
9. Ibid., 252.
10. "England Births and Christenings, 1538–1975 Database," FamilySearch, accessed July 13, 2022, https://familysearch.org/ark:/61903/1:1:JMG1-N52
11. FamilySearch, accessed July 13, 2022, https://www.familysearch.org/tree/person/details/L6N1-P2W.
12. "UK, Prison Commission Records, 1770–1951," Ancestry, accessed July 13, 2022, https://www.ancestry.com.au/imageviewer/collections/61810/images/61810_pcom2_180-00233?treeid=&personid=&hintid=&queryId=79a0c0eb2a794e3d54926e5528d6af04&usePUB=true&_phsrc=AvW2981&_phstart=successSource&usePUBJs=true&_ga=2.206240342.419159320.1617527302-1279535119.1546417886&_gac=1.21017289.1614477214.Cj0KCQiA-OeBBhDiARIsADyBcE6_PrAQq5ILUVXzoRsTMMrXVeRpJKQ5bMdyYg_mY_VLEdMcsj9FEAkaAhjJEALw_wcB&pId=626307&lang=en-AU.
13. David Wells, *The Thames River Police* (London: West India Committee, 2017), 12.
14. Ibid.
15. Ibid., 18.
16. NJB Plomley and K. Henley, "The Sealers of Bass Strait and the Cape Barren Island Community," *Tasmanian Historical Research Association*, 1990, Vol. 37, 54.
17. Bowden, *Captain James Kelly of Hobart Town*, 23.
18. "Harrington (1796 ship)", Wikipedia, accessed July 13, 2022, https://en.wikipedia.org/wiki/Harrington_(1796_ship)
19. *Historical Records of New South Wales, Vol. 4* (Sydney: Government Printer, 1895), 410.
20. Francois Péron, *King Island and the Sealing Trade 1802* (Canberra: Roebuck Society, 1971), 16.
21. Ibid., 16.
22. Ibid., 8.
23. JCH Gill, "Notes on the Sealing Industry of Early Australia," *Journal of the Royal Historical Society of Queensland*, 1967, Vol. 8, 223.
24. Ibid., 225.
25. Ibid.
26. DR Hainsworth, "Iron Men in Wooden Ships: the Sydney Sealers 1800–1820," *Australian Society for the Study of Labour History*, 1967, Vol. 13, 19.

27. Peter Entwisle, *Taka: A Vignette Life of William Tucker 1784–1817* (Dunedin: Port Daniel Press, 2005), 37.
28. Hainsworth, "Iron Men in Wooden ships", 20.
29. Lynette Russell, *Roving Mariners: Australian Aboriginal Whalers and Sealers in the Southern Oceans, 1790–1870* (Albany: State University of New York Press, 2012), 95.
30. Ibid.
31. Péron, *King Island and the Sealing Trade 1802*, 44.
32. Plomley and Henley, "The Sealers of Bass Strait and the Cape Barren Island Community," 54.
33. *The Sydney Gazette and New South Wales Advertiser,* April 14, 1805, 1.
34. *The Sydney Gazette and New South Wales Advertiser,* December 8, 1805, 2.
35. "New South Wales and Tasmania, Australia Convict Musters, 1806–1849", Ancestry, accessed July 13, 2022, https://www.ancestry.com.au/discoveryui-content/view/308609:1185?tid=&pid=&queryId=1e4bdc96a0835cceaf2e976f972907f3&_phsrc=Kaa8&_phstart=successSource
36. *The Sydney Gazette and New South Wales Advertiser,* November 6, 1808, 2.
37. *The Sydney Gazette and New South Wales Advertiser,* July 30, 1809, 1.
38. *The Sydney Gazette and New South Wales Advertiser,* April 7, 1810, 1.
39. Patsy Cameron, *Grease and Ochre: the Blending of Two Cultures at the Colonial Sea Frontier* (Hobart: Fullers Bookshop Pty Ltd, 2011), 74.
40. Ibid.
41. Plomley and Henley, "The Sealers of Bass Strait and the Cape Barren Island Community," 74.
42. NJB Plomley, *Friendly Mission: the Tasmanian Journals and Papers of George Augustus Robinson 1829–34* (Hobart: Quintus Publishing, 2008), 91.
43. Maggie Walter and Louise Daniels, "Personalising the History Wars: Woretemoeteyenner's story," *International Journal of Critical Indigenous Studies*, 2008, Vol.1, 37.
44. Ibid.
45. Charles Jeffreys, *Van Diemen's Land: Geographical and Descriptive Delineations of the Island of Van Diemen's Land* (London: JM Richardson, 1820), 120.
46. Russell, *Roving Mariners,* 17–18.
47. Ibid., 19.
48. Walter and Daniels, "Personalising the History Wars," 37.
49. Plomley, *Friendly Mission,* 327.
50. Ibid.
51. Alison Alexander, *Corruption and Skullduggery: Edward Lord, Maria Riseley and Hobart's Tempestuous Beginnings* (Dynnyrne: Pillinger Press, 2015), 133.
52. *Hobart Town Gazette and Southern Reporter,* July 19, 1819, 1.
53. *The Sydney Gazette and New South Wales Advertiser*, October 2, 1819, 3.
54. Plomley and Henley, "The Sealers of Bass Strait and the Cape Barren Island Community," 74.
55. Geneanet, accessed July 13, 2022, https://gw.geneanet.org/alisontassie?lang=en&p=george+william+christopher+lamuel&n=briggs

56. FamilySearch, accessed July 13, 2022, https://www.familysearch.org/tree/person/details/L6N1-P2W.
57. Julie Gough, *Fugitive History: the Art of Julie Gough* (Perth: UWAP, 2018), 15.
58. Ibid., 266.

Port Arthur or Carnarvon

The changing landscape of a former penal settlement

SARAH WHITE

> "A wonderful and mysterious place was Port Arthur in the eyes of all who had not had the 'good fortune' to visit that portion of her Majesty's domains, either by compulsion or otherwise."
> —G Gruncell, writing as 'Riegel'[1]

On the night of December 26, 1896, a formal ceremony was held to mark the official reopening of the Carnarvon Town Hall. Destroyed by fire almost two years before, the townspeople were excited for the occasion. The hall was lit up for the first time since rebuilding was complete, and a crowd gathered outside waiting impatiently for the doors to open when they could rush in to claim the best vantage for the evening concert.[2]

It was Boxing Day, the day of the traditional wood chopping carnival, and spirits were already high, but combined with optimism for the future, it was to be a night to remember. The Town Hall represented the stability of the bucolic coastal town, and at this time, the future of Carnarvon looked bright.

By all accounts, Reverend Woollnough, MHA performed the official ceremony with great aplomb. He thanked the building contractors, complimented the architect, but most importantly acknowledged the history of the building.[3] For Carnarvon was once known as Port Arthur, and the town hall was once the convict asylum.

Carnarvon Town Hall or Convict Asylum Clock Tower
Sarah White

When Governor George Arthur wrote to the Colonial Secretary, John Burnett, in December 1827, seeking to replace the timber cutting establishment at Birchs Bay, it is unlikely he could have presumed the historical impact of directing an officer to examine "Stewarts Harbour" and to report upon the location.[4]

The site was found agreeable, and Stewart's Harbour was soon named Port Arthur, in honour of Governor Arthur. Established in 1830, the Port Arthur Penal Station operated for some 47 years as a place of secondary punishment. When the last of the convicts departed the site onboard the Harriet on September 17, 1877, the abandonment of the Port Arthur penal station was complete.[5] No one could have anticipated that only months later, the former penal settlement's burgeoning career as a convict tourist attraction would commence. The buildings stood empty, yet tourists soon came in increasing numbers. These visitors, to the newly named town of Carnarvon, were able to experience the very same Port Arthur the convicts saw.

The first of the chartered steamers bearing sightseeing passengers arrived on Boxing Day 1877, carrying 900 passengers in aid of the Manchester Unity International Order of Oddfellows Widows' and Orphans' Fund.[6]

Subsequent charters followed, until 1891 when demand saw a bi-weekly steamer service commence operation between Hobart and Norfolk Bay.[7] Regardless of the form of transport, visitors continued to flock to the former penal settlement to hear of its macabre past. The caretaker, a former Port Arthur convict, turned settlement constable, reportedly supplemented his government income by providing tours of the settlement with his firsthand experience of the times now past.[8]

■

When you speak of Port Arthur, the first thing most people think of is convict history or tragedy. Whichever way you look at it, Port Arthur is a place defined by its dark past. The place is haunted by ghosts, as some would say, both literal and figurative. This, however, hasn't always been the case. Between 1877 and 1927, the town of Port Arthur was known as Carnarvon, and Carnarvon was a town optimistic about its future.

Despite the almost insatiable curiosity of tourists, the township's population was not so quick to grow. It could be suggested this was due to the lingering stain of the convict past, preventing people from wanting to be associated with the area. The convict history of Van Diemen's Land was a contentious issue for those who, like a nameless gentleman, thought the best solution was to put a "quantity of dynamite or gunpowder" under some of the most infamous buildings at Port Arthur.[9]

Realistically, it was the isolation, ideal for the segregation of convicts, but inconvenient for ease of access, which made likely inhabitants hesitant to relocate.[10] Until a road was formed in 1908, the only way to Carnarvon was via a sea voyage.[11] Moving to Carnarvon was an undertaking, but it was one that people became willing to take as access and amenities improved.

In the immediate years following the closure of the settlement, little changed for the town of Carnarvon. Timber merchant Henry Chesterman sent workers to the region, and soon further inhabitants moved to the district.[12] There was little physical change to the settlement. It wasn't until 1884, with the devastating fire at the convict-built church, that the beginning of changes to the penal landscape started to occur.[13]

Notwithstanding the words of the nameless gentlemen with a mind tending towards explosives, the townspeople of Carnarvon came to appreciate the sociocultural significance of their environment. They took pride in the importance of the region's history to their burgeoning township, and not only as the primary drawcard to local tourism. Tourists visited the region due to their curiosity of the convict past and the stunning coastal scenery. The locals appreciated the history for what it could bring to their future.

■

When the colonial government proposed a sale of significant allotments in 1889, with the condition that purchasers demolish and remove structures, Tasmanians were unimpressed.[14] A government minister went so far as to suggest that retaining the buildings as a monument to the past was both "repugnant" and a "disgrace to the British Government."[15] Locals, however, saw the former convict buildings as part of their environment.

Included in the sale were the Separate Prison and the Penitentiary, the two largest buildings of the former penal settlement.[16] A petition was launched to save the buildings that were a significant part of the landscape.[17] Many of these buildings were in a ruinous state, with the building materials worth more than the standing structure. The colonial government was insistent the sale go ahead, which it did but with altered conditions of sale no longer requiring the demolition or removal of the buildings. Regardless, many listings passed in at the auction and the landscape remained unchanged.[18]

The town prospered, the population grew, and with increasing numbers of tourists visiting each season the future of Carnarvon looked assured.

■

It was the major fires of the 1890s that reshaped the former convict landscape beyond recognition, turning the town into a hollow ruin.

On the morning of Friday, January 25, 1895, the first of the great fires swept through Carnarvon.[19] Unlike the accidental fire that destroyed the church in 1884, this fire was the result of an out of control bush fire. Hampered by strong north-westerly winds, the settlement stood little chance of survival. Within no time at all, the former Government Cottage was lost to flames, quickly followed by the former Parsonage, then known as Lightwood House. The former convict Asylum, then used as the Town Hall, the former Hospital, Model Prison, and several private residences were also lost.[20]

When the steamer Nubeena left Taranna that day, it was reported that "the fire was raging, the residents being totally unable to cope with it".[21] Fires were still burning in a number of buildings as late as Saturday evening.[22]

Summer in Tasmania brings with it the risk of fire, and it was not so long after the rebuilding work at Carnarvon was complete that the town was again threatened with danger.

On Thursday, December 30, 1897, Mr Darley, a visitor to the Carnarvon Hotel, the former Commandant's Residence, reported: "… fires on the hills all round".[23] The proprietors of the establishment having firsthand knowledge of the devastation wrought by fires in the local area would have warned their guests of the potential dangers. Mr Darley noted that with the hot north-westerly winds from the previous day still blowing, and with the fires still encircling the region, that "alarm of danger to the township raised, and we, from the hotel, packed our goods and sent them down to the stone jetty".[24] He went on to describe seeing the first burning embers land on the Penitentiary, which quickly spread to all but destroy the former penal settlement.

> Air almost suffocating with heat and dense black smoke. At 4.30 p.m., when standing on the stone jetty, we saw some burning leaves blown from … [the] opposite side of the harbor [*sic*], and fall on the roof of the Penitentiary, quickly followed with more, and within ten minutes the whole roof was on fire and the building doomed.[25]

The fire spread in quick succession from the Penitentiary to nearby structures. The Police Office was lost, followed by Trenham's Boarding House, where Mr Trenham sadly lost his life. Rose Cottage, located alongside the Carnarvon Hotel, and then used as the local school caught alight, followed by a number of other private residences located around the region. The Hospital, rebuilt after the 1895 fires, was again lost. Numerous other structures in the surrounding area fell victim to the flames.[26] The damage, both personal and financial, was simply immeasurable.

> The fire at the Penitentiary, which was the first to take place, was also the last to go out. It became extinguished at 4 o'clock Sunday afternoon, having burned exactly 48 hours.[27]

A number of buildings survived the fires unscathed. There was no further damage to the newly rebuilt Town Hall, nor the buildings still standing today on Officer's Row. The Carnarvon Hotel was spared, as was Exile's Cottage, now more familiarly known as Smith O'Brien's Cottage, despite the close proximity of fires near to both buildings. Despite work undertaken to mitigate risks, fire is both unpredictable and indiscriminatory.

Mr Darley concluded his account of the fires by stating, "Thus ended the year 1897, and almost the last of this once famous penal establishment."[28] Which was likely a belief that many at the time shared. With visitors coming to experience the convict past, and the convict landscape left in ruins, there were concerns for the viability of the town's future.

■

With the sensibilities of Tasmanians torn between those who saw the convict legacy of the colony as a dark stain upon their past, and those who were looking towards a future based heavily on the commodification of said history, the future of the Carnarvon township was seemingly at an impasse.

The tourists, however, continued to arrive. On Monday, January 3, 1898, just days after the fire, 600 visitors arrived for "pleasure and sightseeing".[29] A correspondent reported to *The Mercury*, contrasting the excitement of the tourists and the devastation to the landscape of Carnarvon.

> As the *S.S. Manapouri* steamed into the port yesterday the blue smoke of bush fires rose here and there in thick clouds as if proceeding from a number of independent fires, though it was probable they were all connected in a latent way.[30]

Yet the reports of the fire were quickly disregarded, with the author painting a picture of those who had arrived waiting and expecting to be entertained.

> But, let us get ashore with these 600 people who have come from town with the *Manapouri* with the twofold object of pleasure and sight-seeing. The pleasure seekers pure and simple appear to be numerous enough. They are easily distinguishable from the sight-seers. They sit on the grass in the shade of a tree—an oak from England or a willow from St. Helens—to feast, in view of the desolation around![31]

The desolation that the 600 visitors arriving days after the fire saw was thankfully not to last. Like after the fires that devastated the landscape, the townspeople went to work to rebuild where possible. After the fires, not all destroyed buildings were as fortunate as the Carnarvon Town Hall, the former convict Asylum, rebuilt after the first fire and spared by the second. Dwelling houses were repaired or rebuilt by those who had the means, others sought new accommodations. Lightwood House, once a grand Georgian building was rebuilt on a smaller scale. The former Government Cottage, however, still stands as a ruin. The hospital, rebuilt after the first fire, was left in ruin after the second fire. Rose Cottage, a former officer's residence and later the free school, was razed. The government-owned penitentiary was left as a ruin, along with the privately-owned model prison. The Police Office, the former Law Courts and Commandant's Office, was rebuilt on a larger scale and used as the first iteration of the Hotel Arthur (this building, however, was again lost to fire some years later).[32]

∎

With the former convict landscape merely softened, not erased, the region became more accessible to those who feared the supposed stain of the convict past. The convict landscape was altered, yet still recognisable. The ruins softened the once intimidating structures, making them more accessible to those who thought the shame of Tasmania's convict past too great to bear.[33] It was this combination of ruins and thriving town that made Port Arthur the tourist attraction it is today.[34] Instead of being demolished, the ruins were made use of by the growing tourism industry.

These ruins cemented the growing tourist industry at Port Arthur, slowly killing the town of Carnarvon, and leaving it to be left forgotten in the past. It is the ruins left by these fires that the hundreds of thousands of yearly visitors are most familiar with today.

With the creation of the Scenery Preservation Board in 1915 and the formal appointment of official tour guides, the future of Port Arthur was assured, as the town of Carnarvon slowly was erased. By 1927 the name of Carnarvon was formally reverted to Port Arthur.

∎ ∎ ∎

NOTES

1. Riegel (G Gruncell), "Convict Port Arthur," *The Clipper,* April 22, 1893, 4; http://nla.gov.au/nla.news-article83365241, accessed August 10, 2022.
2. "Port Arthur," *The Mercury,* December 30, 1896, 4; http://nla.gov.au/nla.news-article9388504, accessed August 10, 2022.
3. "Port Arthur," 4.
4. Lieut.-Governor Arthur to John Burnett, Colonial Secretary, 3 December 1827, Tasmanian Archives, CSO1/1/217/5215.

5. "Port Arthur Establishment Report," *Journals of the House of Assembly, Tasmania, No. 56 (1878)*: 3.
6. D Young, "Profiting from the Past: The Relationship Between History and the Tourist Industry in Tasmania 1856–1972', (PhD thesis, University of Tasmania, 1995), 41.
7. M de la Torre, *Heritage Values in Site Management, Four Case Studies,* (Los Angeles: Getty Conservation Institute, 2005), 120.
8. Young, "Profiting," 67.
9. "Great fire at Port arthur" *The Mercury,* January 4, 1898, 3; http://nla.gov.au/nla.news-article9412561, accessed August 25, 2022.
10. Young, "Profiting," 64.
11. JM Crozier, "Innovation at heritage tourist attractions", (PhD thesis, University of Tasmania, 2013), 111.
12. Peter Macfie, "Changes and Continuations: The Post-Penal Settlement of Tasman Peninsula, 1877–1914", (Report: Port Arthur Conservation Project, 1989), 4.
13. NE Goc, "From convict prison to the Gothic ruins of tourist attraction," *Historic Environment*, Vol. 16, no. 3 (2002): 24.
14. Young, "Profiting," 74.
15. Ibid., 74.
16. Ibid., 73.
17. Ibid., 74.
18. "Port Arthur Gaol buildings" *The Mercury,* March 7, 1889, 3; http://nla.gov.au/nla.news-article9207974, accessed August 14, 2022.
19. "The fire at Port Arthur" *The Mercury,* January 29, 1895, *2;* http://nla.gov.au/nla.news-article9311355, accessed August 14, 2022.
20. "Fire at Port Arthur *The Tasmanian*, February 2, 1895, 39; http://nla.gov.au/nla.news-article199066541, accessed August 14, 2022.
21. Ibid., 39.
22. "The fire" 2.
23. CW Darley, "Port Arthur" *Tasmanian News,* January 8, 1898, 2; http://nla.gov.au/nla.news-article173660096, accessed August 15, 2022.
24. Ibid., 2.
25. Ibid., 2.
26. "The Fire at Port Arthur," *Zeehan and Dundas Herald,* January 7, 1898, 4; http://nla.gov.au/nla.news-article84660281, accessed August 15, 2022.
27. "Great fire" 3.
28. Ibid.
29. Ibid.
30. Ibid.
31. Ibid.
32. Carla Howarth, "Port Arthur's hotel sprung up from ruins and once housed Hollywood royalty," March 4, 2020, https://www.abc.net.au/news/2020-03-04/port-arthur-hotel-was-roaring-in-the-post-convict-1920s/11969786, accessed August 15, 2022.
33. Goc, "From convict prison," 24.
34. Crozier, "Innovation," 46.

www.ingramcontent.com/pod-product-compliance
Lightning Source LLC
Chambersburg PA
CBHW061138010526
44107CB00069B/2983